POSITIVE & ENCOURAGING

Positive and Encouraging Thoughts for Women: 90 Devotions of Hope, Strength, and Grace for Your Journey

Published by K-LOVE Books, a partner of Forefront Books, Nashville, Tennessee.
Distributed by Simon & Schuster.

Library of Congress Control Number: 2025914150

Print ISBN: 978-1-63763-510-0
E-book ISBN: 978-1-63763-511-7
Cover Design by Greg Jackson/Thinkpen Design
Interior Design by Jeff Jansen | Aesthetic Soup
Printed in the United States of America

25 26 27 28 29 30 VEP 10 9 8 7 6 5 4 3 2 1

POSITIVE & ENCOURAGING *thoughts for women*

90 DEVOTIONS OF *HOPE*, *STRENGTH*,
AND *GRACE* FOR YOUR JOURNEY

K-LOVE BOOKS

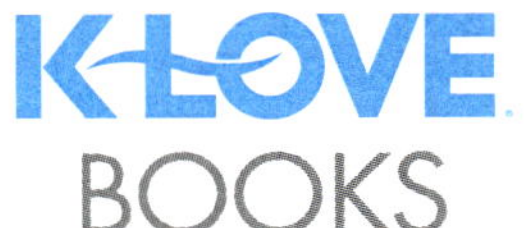

A Message to Readers

Thoughts are intensely powerful things. Your thoughts have the power to lift you up or to drag you down; they have the power to energize you or to deplete you, to inspire you to greater accomplishments or to make those accomplishments impossible.

If you're like most women, you have a busy schedule and a maxed-out to-do list. As a result, you probably have quite a few things that are occupying your thoughts. You may worry about your family, your finances, your career, your health, or your future, for starters. You may feel trapped in a web of personal or social media entanglements, or you may be laboring under the misconception that you must do everything perfectly to meet societal standards that are, in truth, impossible to attain. Or perhaps, you're plagued by vague anxieties that are keeping you up (at night) or holding you back (in life). If so, this book is intended to help.

This text contains a collection of positive and encouraging devotional readings for women—women like you—who understand that when it comes to solving life's existential challenges, God's Word is the final word. And because of His grace, you are loved, you are chosen, and you are enough.

As you consider your own circumstances, remember this: Whatever the size of your challenge, whatever the scope of your problem, God is bigger. Much bigger. And He will instruct you, protect you, energize you, and heal you *if* you let Him. So pray fervently, listen carefully, and treat every single day as an opportunity for praise and thanksgiving because that's what every day can be and should be.

The Bible teaches us to guard our thoughts against things that are hurtful or wrong (Proverbs 4:23). Yet sometimes our emotions can be hijacked by everyday stressors or by the general negativity that seems to characterize twenty-first-century life. If we are to think better thoughts and reap a full measure of God's blessings, we need tools to help us guard our minds and our hearts.

The ideas in this book are intended to help you think constructively about yourself, your circumstances, your faith, and your future. So, if you occasionally find yourself mired in the mental quicksand of pessimism or doubt, it's time to change those thoughts, and step-by-step, life will begin to slowly transform. And today is a great day to start.

8 Principles for Thinking Positive Thoughts

1. **Stay Spiritually Grounded**: Spend time with God every day, pray about big decisions, and listen carefully to your conscience. The enemy wants you to behave impulsively and make poor decisions; God wants you to behave rationally and make wise decisions. Trust God and seek wise counsel.

2. **Monitor Your Thoughts and Reject the Exaggerated Beliefs That Lead to Unproductive Thinking**: Not all thoughts are created equal. A simple way to improve the quality of your thoughts is to recognize—and then make the conscious effort to reject—irrational, exaggerated, or unhelpful thoughts. So, if you can tell your thoughts are heading in the wrong direction, slow down, take a few deep breaths, say a prayer, and replace those counterproductive thoughts with positive ones.

3. **Be a Realistic Optimist**: In the journey of life, chronic pessimism is a dead-end street. So don't invent imaginary catastrophes and be open to the possibility that good things will happen, and soon. Foster a realistic sense of self-confidence and avoid worst-case thinking. Whatever your circumstances, say no to pessimism and yes to hope.

4. **Make Peace with Your Past and Forgive Everybody**: Bitterness is intellectual poison. If you remain stuck in

the past, you'll spoil the present and sabotage the future. So forgive everybody (including yourself) immediately and permanently. And if you can't seem to forgive, keep praying about it until you can.

5. **Accept the Things You Cannot Change and Focus on the Things You Can Change**: Refuse to fret, obsess, or remain solely focused on things you can't control. Instead, divide your concerns into two categories: the things you can change and the things you can't. After you've made that determination, get to work on the things that are in your control and let God take care of the rest.

6. **Learn How to Control Your Emotions Before They Control You:** Exaggerated thoughts have a way of revving up your emotions. And emotional outbursts can have bitter consequences. So if you feel your emotional temperature beginning to rise, call time-out before they burst, not after. True wisdom is knowing how and when to step away from a combustible situation before it ignites.

7. **Be Thankful and Learn to Live in the Present:** Learn to focus on your blessings, not your hardships. The Lord has given you more blessings than you can count. And while you're trying to make a list of God's gifts, remember Psalm 118:24: "This is the day the LORD has made; We will rejoice and be glad in it" (NKJV).

8. **If Your Thoughts Seem Seriously Distorted, Seek Help ASAP:** Sometimes, faulty thinking has physiological causes. Thankfully, medical conditions like depression or bipolar disorder are readily treatable. So if there's any question about the state of your mental health, seek help immediately.

1

Redirecting Your Thoughts

Fix your thoughts on what is true, and honorable, and right, and pure, and lovely, and admirable. Think about things that are excellent and worthy of praise.

PHILIPPIANS 4:8 NLT

As women, we are always busy with our thoughts. We simply can't avoid them. Because of our many responsibilities, our brains never shut off—and even while we're sleeping, we mull things over. The question is not *if* we will think; the question is *how* we will think and *what* we will think about.

Jesus understood the burden of having worries and responsibilities. When He told us not to worry, it was not to scold us but to reassure us that God loves us and is in control (Matthew 6:25–34). When we spend too much time dwelling on the uncertainties of tomorrow, we lose sight of the peace in the present moment. But directing our thoughts in a more positive direction robs our worries of the power to control us.

The American poet Phoebe Cary observed, "All the great blessings of my life are present in my thoughts today." These words can also apply to you and me. When you find yourself overwhelmed by your swirling and troubled thoughts, try redirecting your thoughts toward your blessings. Form an optimistic vision in your mind about the world you live in and the life you lead. Then, prepare yourself for the blessings that good thoughts will bring.

Thinking Positive Thoughts

Our thoughts have the power to lift us up or bring us down—but the good news is, we are more in control of our minds than we think! Thankfully, we can improve the quality of our lives by making mental adjustments. If your inner voice is your inner critic, try toning down or even tuning out the criticism. If you find yourself envisioning negative outcomes, try envisioning a positive one instead. Ask God to help you reframe your thinking if you feel yourself falling into a familiar pattern of worry. With His help, we can all train ourselves to begin thinking thoughts that are healthier and clear-sighted, more accepting, and less judgmental. Try looking at yourself through the eyes of God.

Remember This

Unbridled thoughts have the power to lift your spirits or bring them down. Instead of letting them run wild, ask God to guide and direct you as you learn to reframe and control your thoughts. With His gentle leading and care, your negative and worrisome thoughts will have no power over you.

Being grateful and living in the spirit of gratitude automatically reminds you of the greatness of God.

CeCe Winans

2

Doing Life with God

The Lord *is my shepherd;*
I have all that I need . . .
He renews my strength.
He guides me along right paths.
Psalm 23:1, 3 NLT

Because He made you and loves you, you will always have some type of relationship with God. But for a person of faith, the question is not *if* you will have a relationship with Him; the question is whether that relationship will be one that seeks to honor and respect Him and His purpose for your life.

One easy and sure way to grow in your faith is to do so with God as your partner, father, best friend, and guide. When you put God first in every aspect of your life, you'll be comforted by the knowledge that His wisdom is ultimate and His plans are the best for you. When you invite God into your decisions and your dreams, your outlook will change, your priorities will change, and your behaviors will change—for the better. When you go to Him first amid your worries and concerns, you'll experience the genuine peace and lasting comfort that only He can give.

Thankfully, the Lord is always available to His children. He's always ready to listen, and He's waiting to hear from you now.

Thinking Positive Thoughts

To minimize your worries and maximize your joy, focus on this thought: *God deserves first place in my life.* Then, for a few moments, search your heart for the thoughts, concerns, and plans you have not surrendered to God. Spend some time sharing what you've found with God in prayer. Listen for His loving direction and thank Him for always leading you down the right paths.

Remember This

When we allow temptations or distractions to come between us and our Creator, we suffer. But, when we place the Lord at the center of our lives—consulting Him every day and at every important turn—we will be blessed today, tomorrow, and forever by His wisdom and loving-kindness.

God wants to be in our leisure time as much as He is in our churches and in our work.

BETH MOORE

3

Trusting the Lord When Times Are Tough

All praise to God, the Father of our Lord Jesus Christ. God is our merciful Father and the source of all comfort. He comforts us in all our troubles so that we can comfort others. When they are troubled, we will be able to give them the same comfort God has given us.

2 Corinthians 1:3–4 NLT

The Bible promises us that tough times are temporary, but God's love is not; His love endures forever. What does that mean for you and me? From time to time, everybody faces disappointment, confusion, pain, and other suffering. And when those tough times arrive, God stands ready to protect and heal His children.

Psalm 147:3 promises that God cares for the brokenhearted, but we are not promised instant healing. Usually, it takes time—and maybe even a little help from you—for God to fix things. If you're facing tough times, ask God to support you and guide you. If you find yourself in any kind of trouble, pray about your concerns and then ask for wisdom and understanding. The Lord will work things out, just as He has promised—but He will do it in His own way and in His own time.

Thinking Positive Thoughts

The next time you experience tough times (and you will), try to remember the story of Hannah, found in 1 Samuel 1–2. For years,

Hannah grieved that she had never had a child. Yet God saw Hannah and her patient, diligent prayers—and at the right time, He granted her a son named Samuel.

God may not answer our prayers in ways we hope or expect—but to believe in God's goodness and righteousness makes a big difference in the way we face our problems. When tempted by discouragement, try not to give in. Instead, open your heart to God, pray diligently, and expect the best from Him. God is always with you, and you are always protected.

Remember This

Amid tough times, don't hit the panic button. Keeping everything bottled up inside doesn't help either. While you're waiting for answers to prayer, find a trustworthy believer and talk things over. We were meant to share our burdens with one another. And a second opinion or, for that matter, a third or fourth, can often be helpful too. It takes a community!

Regardless of how God answers, I know that He hears my prayers, and He sees my needs.

MANDISA

4

Making Daily Appointments with God

Morning by morning he wakens me and opens my understanding to his will. The Sovereign LORD has spoken to me, and I have listened.

ISAIAH 50:4–5 NLT

Want to worry less and enjoy life more? If so, try spending a few minutes with God every morning.

Each new day is a gift from above. What better way to enjoy that gift than to spend a few quiet moments each morning thanking the Giver?

When we begin each day with heads bowed and hearts lifted, we remind ourselves of God's love, will, protection, and commandments. Spending time in prayer or meditation over His Word helps us align our priorities for the coming day with the teachings He has given us. Further, dwelling in God's presence before the busyness of the day—even if only for a few moments— can calm our spiraling thoughts and fill us with a fortifying peace to carry us through whatever the day has to offer.

Are you seeking to change or improve some aspect of your life? Are you hoping to draw nearer to the Father? If so, ask for His help and ask for it many times each day, starting with your morning appointment with God.

Thinking Positive Thoughts

To organize your thoughts and prepare for the coming day, resolve to make a regular appointment with your Creator. God is ready to talk to you!

Try not to think of your appointment with God as something that lengthens your to-do list. Instead, think of this time as a gift to yourself, whether it be thirty minutes or three.

Spend your devotional time over coffee, in a comfortable chair, or in your coziest robe and slippers. Light a candle and play some calming music if that creates an atmosphere of peace for you.

If you are short on time, consider whether you can turn your morning commute into a moment of quiet prayer and meditation. And, of course, you can always set your appointments for later in the day. Maybe you and God can spend some time together as you're folding laundry or taking a walk. God wants to hear from you—anytime, anywhere, under any circumstances.

Remember This

A regular time of quiet reflection and prayer will offer you the perfect opportunity to praise your Creator and focus your thoughts. There are no rules for this time between you and God—so don't let the pressure to "get it right" come between you and your sacred moments with Him.

Never is a woman so fulfilled as when she chooses to underwhelm her schedule so she can let God overwhelm her soul.

Lysa TerKeurst

Entrusting the Future to God

You will keep in perfect peace all who trust in you,
all whose thoughts are fixed on you!

Isaiah 26:3 NLT

As every woman knows, hope is a perishable commodity. Despite God's promises, despite Christ's love, and despite our countless blessings, we can still lose hope when setbacks happen from time to time. When we do lose our hope, we need the encouragement of Christian friends, the life-changing power of prayer, and the healing truth of God's holy Word. In other words, we need regular reminders that we can trust the God who made us and loves us.

The Bible teaches that the Lord blesses those who trust in His wisdom and follow in the footsteps of His Son. God's Word also teaches us that He is faithful to keep His promises (Psalm 145:13). The promises He has made are important—nothing short of *eternal* importance! So when you trust God with your hopes, dreams, and plans, you'll have every reason on earth—and in heaven—to be hopeful about your future.

Next time you notice despair creeping in, dwell on all God has done for you rather than on a multitude of formidable what-ifs. Be optimistic, be faithful, and do your best. Then leave the rest to God. Your destiny is safe with Him.

Thinking Positive Thoughts

To remind yourself of God's eternal faithfulness, write the following words on a sticky note and place it somewhere you'll see it regularly (such as your bathroom mirror, the dashboard of your car, or the front of your planner or journal):

God has promised to guide and protect me, today and forever.

For other sticky noteworthy promises of God, consider writing down some of the words from Psalm 9:10, Isaiah 54:10, and Hebrews 10:23. Let these reminders bring you peace and comfort whenever you see them.

For the mountains may move, but even then, my faithful love for you will remain.

Hold tightly without wavering, for God can be trusted to keep his promise.

Remember This

If you're experiencing hard times, look for ways to spend more time with God. And never be afraid to hope—or to ask—for a miracle.

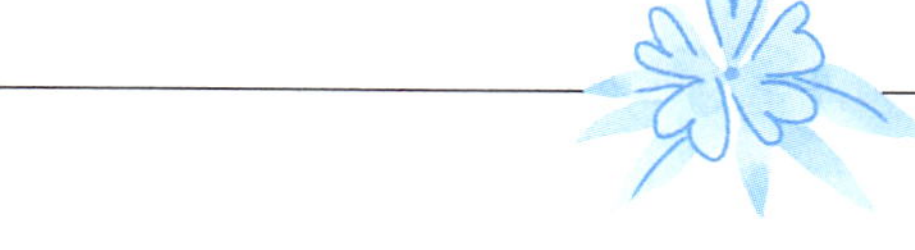

Hope looks for the good in people, opens doors for people, discovers what can be done to help, lights a candle, does not yield to cynicism. Hope sets people free.

Barbara Johnson

6

Keep on Praying

Rejoice in our confident hope.
Be patient in trouble, and keep on praying.
ROMANS 12:12 NLT

Prayer is a powerful tool that can change us *and* change the world. God hears every prayer and responds in His own way and according to His own schedule and plan. When you make a habit of consulting Him about everything, He'll guide you along a path of His choosing—which is the path you should take. And when you petition Him for strength, He'll give you the courage to face any problem and the ability to meet any challenge.

Continual prayer also changes the quality of your thoughts and the direction of your day. So today, instead of turning things over in your mind, turn them over to God in prayer. Take your concerns to the Lord and leave them in His capable hands. Your heavenly Father is listening, and He wants to hear from you.

Thinking Positive Thoughts

Faithful women of the Bible such as Hannah, Esther, and Deborah have modeled what it looks like to pray with thanksgiving and praise. Perhaps the most famous prayer is the "Magnificat," the song sung by Jesus's mother, Mary, upon learning she would be bringing God's Son into the world. Found in Luke 1:46–55, her powerful and beautiful words document her belief in the Father and her faith in His surprising plans for her life.

What would your own version of Mary's "Magnificat" look and sound like? Consider writing your own version to God, using the words and feelings that feel most true to you.

Remember This

If you find yourself overwhelmed or stressed or anxious, find a quiet place and pray about your situation. Ask God for His peace and guidance and ask Him for the courage to meet the challenges ahead. Rest assured that when you ask, He answers.

Pour out your heart to the Father
and seek first the kingdom of God.

TASHA LAYTON

7

Avoiding Distractions That Attack Your Heart

Let us lay aside every weight, and the sin which so easily ensnares us, and let us run with endurance the race that is set before us.

Hebrews 12:1 NKJV

All of us experience days when traffic jams and computer glitches seem to be clamoring for our time and attention. Our kids catch colds, tires go flat, or we realize at the end of the workday that we've forgotten an important deadline. But when we find ourselves overwhelmed by the minor—or major!—frustrations of life, let's take a step back and breathe, and lift our thoughts upward.

Although we may struggle to rise above the distractions of everyday living, we need not struggle alone. God is here—eternal and faithful, with infinite patience and love—and, if we reach out to Him, He will restore our sense of perspective and give peace to our souls.

Thinking Positive Thoughts

Take a few minutes to consider the way you tend to respond to the obstacles that pop up in front of you. Is your instinct to panic, or is your instinct to pray?

If you need a gentle nudge to turn your thoughts toward God, consider setting yourself a daily reminder on your phone. Schedule a little check-in with God at a time of day that tends to be particularly hectic. Even a few short breaths and a few words of prayer may be enough to help reset your spirit.

Remember This

The world is filled with enough distractions to keep us occupied for years—but our challenge is to turn our ears toward Jesus. As we spend time in His holy presence and dwell on His promises, the distractions that once screamed for our attention may soon fade noiselessly into the background.

Trust and thankfulness will get you safely through this day. Trust protects you from worrying and obsessing. Thankfulness keeps you from criticizing and complaining.

Sarah Young

8

Doing the Important Work—Now

When you make a promise to God, don't delay in following through, for God takes no pleasure in fools. Keep all the promises you make to him.

Ecclesiastes 5:4 NLT

The old saying is both familiar and true: Actions speak louder than words. And as believers, we know from Scripture that "faith without good deeds is useless" (James 2:20 NLT). Our actions should always give credence to the changes that Christ can make in the lives of those who walk with Him.

God calls upon each of us to act in accordance with His will and with respect for His commandments. But knowing what Scripture says is only one step of the journey. As followers of Jesus, we should not only *know* the instructions of God but also strive to live by them—following Him in word *and* deed.

God doesn't need our help, but He has graciously invited us into the work He is accomplishing on earth. When we serve Him and our neighbors, our loving heavenly Father rewards our efforts with a bountiful harvest. The best part of working on behalf of the kingdom is the honor of working in partnership with God Himself, the Creator. What could be more rewarding than that?

Thinking Positive Thoughts

Today resolve to take action toward something as soon as the idea to do so crosses your mind. Make the call to that friend you've been missing. Invite your neighbor over for tea. Send that note of encouragement. Sign up for that retreat you've been thinking about. If you feel hesitant, ask God to give you the courage to move ahead with boldness. Even one small step moves you forward.

Remember This

The habit of procrastination is often rooted in the fear of failure, the fear of discomfort, or the fear of embarrassment. Your challenge is to confront these fears and defeat them. Ask God for help on this front—and He will provide it!

The enemy of progress is often our own hesitation.
When we choose to do the hard things today,
we open the door for God's grace
to work mightily in our lives.

Susie Davis

9

Discovering God's Plan for Your Life

Teach me your ways, O Lord, that I may live according to your truth! Grant me purity of heart, so that I may honor you.

Psalm 86:11 NLT

God has a plan for this world and your life. He understands His plan perfectly—(He came up with it, after all!)—and this flawless, divine plan can bring you untold joy now and throughout eternity. But the Lord won't force His plan upon you. He's given you free will, the ability to make choices on your own. The totality of those choices will determine how you fulfill God's calling.

Sometimes God makes Himself known in obvious ways, but more often, His guidance is subtle. To hear His voice, we may need a quiet place.

If you're serious about discovering—or rediscovering—God's plan for your life, find quiet moments throughout your day and ask Him for direction. Pray for clarity and be watchful for His signs. The more time you spend with Him, the sooner the answers will come.

Thinking Positive Thoughts

God has a plan for your life—a wonderful plan that looks to the future. But sometimes we are too busy focusing on the past to turn our eyes to the path ahead. If you find yourself revisiting your failures or regrets, ask God for the strength to learn from your mistakes and then move forward. Your future is not behind you but before you.

Your goal is to make peace with the past so you may then look boldly toward the future God has in store for you.

Remember This

Sometimes waiting faithfully for God's plan to unfold is more important than understanding the plan itself. Some answers may not be revealed until we are on the other side of this life. Ruth Bell Graham once said, "When I am dealing with an all-powerful, all-knowing God, I, as a mere mortal, must offer my petitions not only with persistence, but also with patience. Someday I'll know why." So even when you can't understand God's plans, ask Him to strengthen your faith and confidence in His divine wisdom.

"When you're on a journey to discover God's plan,
remember that you are loved,
and His plans for you are good."

LYSA TERKEURST

10

Remembering That God Is in Control (So You Don't Have to Be)

"Can you solve the mysteries of God? Can you discover everything about the Almighty? Such knowledge is higher than the heavens—and who are you? It is deeper than the underworld—what do you know? It is broader than the earth and wider than the sea."

Job 11:7–9 NLT

God is sovereign—a King reigning over the entire universe, including your little corner of that universe. As Christians, we recognize God's sovereignty and hope to live in accordance with His commandments. We also endeavor to trust His promises. Sometimes, of course, these tasks are easier said than done.

Your heavenly Father may not always reveal Himself as quickly (or as clearly) as you would like. But rest assured: God is in control. He is here, He loves you and me, and He intends to use us in wonderful, unexpected ways. He desires to lead His children along paths of His choosing. We have the great opportunity to watch, listen, learn, and follow Him—and we can start today, right this very minute.

Thinking Positive Thoughts

Pondering the power and sovereignty of God can be an exercise that leads to trust and awe. Spend a few moments considering how God made a universe so large that no one has observed its edges.

Meditate upon the *trillions* of cells that comprise your body. Then imagine the God who knows what happens to each one. If ever you are feeling confused in your day, consider how God is in control of His infinite universe *and* your finite world. No concern is too small for Him—but neither is any problem too big.

Remember This

Though He rules over the universe, God is not too busy to care about what's happening in *your* world. How incredible is it to know that such a God cares for you and considers you His child (Galatians 3:26)?

You are God's chief creation, and you are here for His pleasure and His glory.

BETH MOORE

11

Connecting with Other Believers

So now you Gentiles are no longer strangers and foreigners. You are citizens along with all of God's holy people. You are members of God's family..

Ephesians 2:19 NLT

Are you a member of a church? Fellowship with other believers can be an immensely rewarding part of your everyday life. Your association with fellow Christians will be uplifting, enlightening, and encouraging when you find a group of friends who will support and pray for you through the ups and downs.

Life can be busy and tiring, but church can be a place to receive support, prayer, and encouragement from people walking through life with you (Hebrews 10:24–25). A church home can provide opportunities for you to glorify God by contributing your time and your talents to a close-knit community of believers. The fellowship of believers is a powerful tool for spreading God's good news and uplifting His children.

God designed us for relationship. Church connects you with a spiritual family where you can belong, serve, and be known. If you are looking for a church home, ask God for guidance as you continue the search. And if you are already a member of a congregation, look to become more involved in ways that feel right and natural to you.

Thinking Positive Thoughts

You need fellowship with men and women of faith. And your Christian friends need fellowship with you. If you would like to be more active in your church, remember that most churches rely on volunteers! Consider volunteering for a team that fits your gifts—greeting guests, taking part in the worship, ministering to children, or planning events that bring the people of God together.

Remember This

If you genuinely want to build a closer relationship with God, try to build closer relationships with godly people who can walk with you through life's journey. They will understand your priorities and help you make godly decisions. And your commitment to fellow Christians, if taken seriously, will likely lead to some of the deepest and most satisfying friendships you've ever had—friendships that could last for eternity!

When you and I understand how loved we are by God—in our best moments and our worst moments—then I think that gives us the security and the foundation to be able to reach out and be a good friend.

Sheila Walsh

12

Doing First Things First

So prepare your minds for action and exercise self-control.

1 Peter 1:13 NLT

Do you ever have trouble prioritizing your day? Perhaps you've been putting out fires one at a time, in whatever order the fires present themselves. Some prefer to use online or paper scheduling systems, while others may hire professional organizers to bring some clarity to the chaos. Each of us makes choices about what matters most in our lives—and sometimes, we forget to ask God for His instruction and guidance.

What if we took a step back and tried to organize our lives around God's plans *first*? A better strategy than struggling through each daily obligation is to take your responsibilities and your to-dos and place them in the hands of the One who created you. Then you can face the day with the assurance that the same God who created our universe out of nothing will help you place first things first in your own life.

If you feel anxious, overwhelmed, or confused, turn the concerns of this day over to the Lord—prayerfully, earnestly, and often. Then listen for His answer and trust the answer He gives.

Thinking Positive Thoughts

What if you could think more clearly and get more done if you began your day with a to-do list that reflects your values and your priorities? Guess what—you can! If you already have a paper calendar, scheduling app, or to-do list in hand, bathe that list in prayer. Then, when the time to act arrives, make things happen. Carve out moments in between (or during) your chores and obligations to check in with God throughout the day. He cares about even your smallest tasks—and He happens to be wonderful company too.

Remember This

Invite God into every task you do, no matter how insignificant it seems. Then, throughout the day, thank God for small blessings—sunshine, a kind word, a good laugh, or a satisfying meal. Gratitude keeps your heart anchored in Him.

How important it is for us—young and old—to live as if Jesus would return any day—to set our goals, make our choices, raise our children, and conduct business with the perspective of the imminent return of our Lord.

Gloria Gaither

13

Having the Courage to Trust God

Trust in the Lord with all your heart; do not depend on your own understanding. Seek his will in all you do, and he will show you which path to take.

PROVERBS 3:5–6 NLT

Harriet Tubman was born into slavery in the early 1800s. Despite the beatings, harsh labor, and unimaginable suffering she endured, she also had a deep faith in God. After escaping slavery, Harriet felt a strong calling to return to harm's way and rescue others, risking her life each time. Most of us know Harriet Tubman as the "engineer" of the Underground Railroad—a system of courageous individuals who helped tens of thousands of enslaved persons find their way to freedom.

Tubman did not take credit for her efforts. Rather, she is famous for saying, "'Twas the Lord!" She confessed to God: "I don't know where to go or what to do, but I expect you to lead me." Her faith and trust in the Father gave her the confidence to do great things for others.

Are you seeking God's blessings for yourself and your family? Trusting Him is the first step toward those blessings. Trust Him with your relationships. Trust Him with your priorities. Follow His commandments and pray for His guidance. Trust your heavenly Father day by day, moment by moment, in good times and in bad times. You may have to wait patiently for His revelations, but in the meantime, prepare yourself for the abundance and peace that will most certainly be yours when you do.

Thinking Positive Thoughts

If you were not afraid, which of your dreams might come to pass? Dwell on this question for a little while. Then consider whether you have invited God into this dream. Has He placed this dream in your heart? And what could happen if you trusted God with this dream of yours?

Remember This

God is your shield and your strength; He is your protector and your deliverer, and He is worthy of your trust. Call upon Him in your hour of need and draw courage from the source of strength that never fails: your heavenly Father.

God really loves us.
That is the core premise of the gospel.

Lisa Harper

14

Persevering like Jesus

So, my dear brothers and sisters, be strong and immovable. Always work enthusiastically for the Lord, for you know that nothing you do for the Lord is ever useless.

1 Corinthians 15:58 NLT

A well-lived life is like a marathon, not a sprint; it calls for preparation, determination, and, of course, lots of perseverance. As a great example of perseverance, we need to look no further than Jesus Christ.

Jesus finished what He began. Despite His suffering and despite the unspeakable pain He experienced on the cross, Jesus was steadfast in His faithfulness to God. How can we, too, remain faithful when we experience the inevitable hardships of life?

If you are living through tough times or facing a difficult situation, just keep putting one foot in front of the other. Each step forward, no matter how small, can be counted as progress. Pray for strength and keep going. For inspiration, think about Jesus, and all those who persevered before you. God carried them through, and He can do the same for you.

Thinking Positive Thoughts

If you're feeling exhausted and as though your work is never done, try making a "done list." Before you go to sleep, set aside the items left on your to-do list and instead count up the small wins of the day. Focusing on what you *have* achieved may give you just enough mental fortitude to calm your mind and wake up ready to take on the next day. Even small successes are worth celebrating.

Remember This

When you are being tested, remember that God can use everything for good. He can give you the strength to persevere, and someday, you will be able to see clearly just how far He carried you.

*When we reach the end of our strength,
wisdom, and personal resources, we enter
into the beginning of his glorious provisions.*

Patsy Clairmont

15

Choosing Generosity

God loves a person who gives cheerfully.
2 Corinthians 9:7 NLT

The theme of generosity is woven into the fabric of God's Word. Our Creator instructs us to give generously—and cheerfully—to those in need. And He promises that when we do give of our time, our talents, and our resources, we will be blessed.

Jesus was the perfect example of generosity. He gave us everything, even His earthly life, so that we might receive abundance, peace, and eternity. He was always generous, always kind, always willing to help "the least of these" (Matthew 25:40 NLT). And, if we are to follow in His footsteps, we, too, must strive to be generous.

Sometime today, you'll encounter someone who needs a helping hand or a word of encouragement. When you encounter a person in need, think of yourself as Christ's ambassador. Focus on thinking generously about that person. Then act in a way toward them that demonstrates the generosity of God. Share with them, speak kind words to them, and refrain from judging them in their moment of need. Remember that whatever you do for the least of these, you also do for Him. We ought to be generous toward others because God has been generous with us.

Thinking Positive Thoughts

There's a direct relationship between generosity and joy: The more you share with others, the more joy you'll experience for yourself. God gave you blessings so you can use them and share them. Today is the right day to use your talents, to share your blessings, and to experience the joy of giving.

Remember This

As recipients of God's blessings and His grace, our work is to share His gifts with others. Today and every day, talk to Him about ways you can serve His children. If you are unsure of where to start, pray for a specific word from Him regarding how you might give of yourself in small and large ways.

God doesn't just want our money.
He wants our hearts.
And when He has our hearts,
He has our resources too.
Giving is an act of worship and an expression
of gratitude for His abundant grace.

Beth Moore

16

Praying for Perspective

Love wisdom like a sister; make insight a beloved member of your family.

Proverbs 7:4 NLT

If a temporary loss of perspective has left you worried, exhausted, or both, you're not alone. Many of us are prone to negative thoughts, which can be habit-forming. Thankfully, so are positive ones.

Though your nature may be to catastrophize or dwell on everything that could possibly go wrong, with practice you can form the habit of focusing on God's priorities and your own possibilities. When you practice shifting your train of thought, you'll soon discover yourself spending less time fretting about your challenges and more time praising God for His gifts.

The Bible tells us that the Lord—the source of all knowledge—freely gives of His wisdom (James 1:5). When you call upon Him and prayerfully seek His will, He will give you the perspective you need. A situation that once filled you with gloom may suddenly feel like an opportunity for growth. A failure or a rejection may set you on a course to something far better than what you'd planned for yourself. So today and every time you feel yourself losing hope, pray for insight and a sense of balance. No problems are too big for God—including yours.

Thinking Positive Thoughts

Does it warm your heart to know you are an integral part of God's grand plan? It should! Setbacks and inconveniences are frustrating, but consider that some frustrations may be part of God's plan too. Only God Himself knows the details of His intentions, but we can take joy in knowing that He has given us divine parts to play.

Remember This

When you focus on the world, you lose perspective. When you focus on God's promises, you gain better vision. Spending time each day studying God's Word and praying about His plans for you are two wonderful ways to recenter your sight line and provide you the perspective you need.

God gave me the desires of my heart,
and then He gave me what He desired for me.
His plan was much better than my own.

Sarah Jakes Roberts

17

Aspiring to Answer God's Call

I . . . beg you to lead a life worthy of your calling, for you have been called by God.

Ephesians 4:1 NKJV

Have you already heard God's call on your life? And if so, are you pursuing it with enthusiasm? Those who have heard and accepted God's call are blessed. But if you have not yet discovered what God intends for you to do with your life, keep searching, seek wise counsel, and keep praying until you discover the Creator's purpose for your life.

In the Old Testament, Queen Esther was in a special position to stand up and speak for her people, who were under threat. Mordecai, her uncle, said to her, "Who knows if perhaps you were made queen for just such a time as this?" (Esther 4:14 NLT). No doubt, God was able to use Esther and her special role as queen to save the nation of Israel.

Likewise, God has important work for you to do—work that no one else on earth can accomplish but you. You exist in a particular location, amid particular people, with unique opportunities to serve. Even more encouraging is the knowledge that He has given you all the tools you need to succeed. So listen for His voice, watch for His signs, and prepare yourself for the call that is sure to come.

Thinking Positive Thoughts

God's divine calling for you need not look like martyrdom or some grandiose, heroic act. Rather, God often uses us for small, faithful acts of quiet service. When you say yes to helping a neighbor, volunteering at church, listening to someone who's hurting, taking care of your family, or simply showing kindness in daily life, you open your heart to God's guidance. If you notice a pattern of joy amid your service, perhaps you have found your divine calling in Him.

Remember This

God has a plan for your life. No one has lived the way you have: no one has lived exactly where you live, had your specific personality or giftings, or built the relationships you have built. In Him, you are one of a kind—and so is your calling.

God never calls without enabling us.
In other words, if he calls you to do something,
he makes it possible for you to do it.

Luci Swindoll

18

Focusing on Possibilities, Not Setbacks

Jesus looked at them intently and said, "Humanly speaking, it is impossible. But with God everything is possible."

MATTHEW 19:26 NLT

Sometimes even the most optimistic women can become discouraged. No one is immune to exhaustion, failure, self-consciousness, or the burden of responsibilities—and everyone understands feeling weak, "less than," or lacking.

But how might our mindsets change if we were determined to spend more time focusing on our strengths rather than our weaknesses? Our successes rather than our mistakes?

Every day, including this one, is brimming with possibilities. Every day is filled with chances to grow, to serve, and to share. But when we focus too long on our latest failures, we may overlook the blessed opportunities for renewal that God has scattered along our paths.

Don't let pessimism, doubt, negativity, or cynicism steal your future triumphs. Instead, fix your heart upon the Creator. Shake off setbacks, learn what you can from them, do your best to move forward, and let Him handle the rest.

Thinking Positive Thoughts

If you are struggling to let go of something that is keeping you from moving forward—a past mistake, a nagging emotion, or something you perceive as a weakness in yourself—spend a little time writing about it in a journal or notebook. Once you've recorded everything you want to say about this roadblock, write down what you have been able to learn from this struggle. Count those lessons as part of your personal growth, thank God for the wisdom you've gained, and ask Him to help you leave the rest behind.

Remember This

With God, all things are possible—so when you assume you are not equipped for what's been set before you, you put limitations on the things He can do! When you are discouraged, try to remember that His power is unlimited. He has already overcome the world (John 16:33).

God's all-sufficiency is a major. Your inability is a minor. Major in majors, not in minors.

CORRIE TEN BOOM

19

Forgiving Everyone and Everything

If you forgive those who sin against you, your heavenly Father will forgive you. But if you refuse to forgive others, your Father will not forgive your sins.

MATTHEW 6:14–15 NLT

The world holds few, if any, rewards for those who remain angrily focused upon past wrongs. Some may find a certain satisfaction in holding a grudge—yet such feelings are short-lived and rarely productive over the long term.

Even so, the act of forgiveness is difficult for most of us.

Are you stuck in a cycle of bitterness or resentment? Does something that happened long ago still have a grip on you? If so, you are falling short of God's hope for you—and you are also wasting your time. You could also be missing the blessings that God has for you by living in the past.

Being frail, fallible, imperfect human beings, most of us are quick to anger, quick to blame, slow to forgive, and even slower to forget. Yet as Christians, Jesus commanded us to forgive others, just as we, too, have been forgiven.

If there exists even one person—alive or dead—against whom you hold bitter feelings, ask yourself, "What will it take for me to forgive? Am I clinging to a harm that's been done, and how can I learn to release it?" Or, if you are embittered against yourself for some past mistake or shortcoming, how might you forgive and carry on? Hatred, bitterness, and regret are not part of God's plan for your life. Ask Him today to help you forgive everyone and everything.

Thinking Positive Thoughts

Bitterness is its own punishment, and forgiveness is its own reward. If you are struggling to forgive someone, visualize how different your life would be without this burden on your heart. How would forgiveness empower you? What would change in your spirit?

Remember This

Today is the perfect day to ask God for strength. Ask Him to help you forgive every single person who has hurt you—and then, as a follower of Jesus, thank Him for forgiving you too.

Forgiveness is weapon. Our choices moving forward are the battlefield. Moving on is the journey. Being released from that heavy feeling is the reward.

LYSA TERKEURST

20

Following Your Conscience

Let us go right into the presence of God with sincere hearts fully trusting him. For our guilty consciences have been sprinkled with Christ's blood to make us clean, and our bodies have been washed with pure water.

Hebrews 10:22 NLT

God has given each of us a conscience, and He intends for us to use it.

A woman following her conscience walks a path of quiet strength and steady conviction. She listens not to the noise of the world but to the gentle prompting of the Holy Spirit within her. Her decisions aren't always popular, but she chooses what is right over what is easy. Whether she's standing up for someone overlooked, refusing to compromise her integrity, or simply choosing kindness in a tense moment, she follows the voice God placed in her heart. Her conscience becomes a compass shaped by Scripture, prayer, and love for others. She may not see the impact right away, but God uses her courage in unseen ways.

But what if we ignore the quiet inner voice that warns us against disobedience and danger? What if we're tempted to rush headlong into situations we soon come to regret?

God promises to reward good conduct and bless those who obey His Word. Wise women run toward that blessing. Count yourself among their number.

Sometime soon, perhaps today, your conscience will speak.

When it does, listen carefully. God may be trying to get a message through to you—a message you desperately need to hear.

Thinking Positive Thoughts

If you listen carefully, that quiet little voice inside your head will guide you down the right path and keep you out of danger. Try to think back on a time when God pinged your conscience. Did you listen and correct your course? Or did you ignore His urging and wind up going the wrong way? Thank Him for each time a gentle nudge from Him has protected you from harm.

Remember This

If you're not sure what to do, slow down and search for silence. It's difficult to listen to your conscience amid so much noise. The little voice inside your heart is remarkably dependable, but you can't depend upon it if you can't hear it. Slow down, listen, and learn from the message your conscience is desperately trying to send.

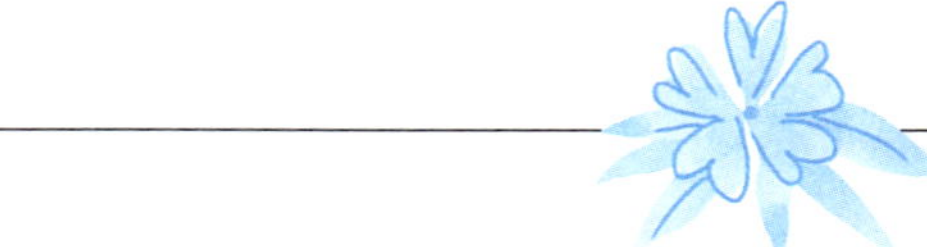

God wired us with an inner voice that
whispers His truth and direction.
We must learn to quiet the noise around us to hear it.

PRISCILLA SHIRER

21

Making God's Priorities Your Priorities

Come close to God, and God will come close to you.

James 4:8 NLT

Have you asked God to help prioritize your life? Have you asked Him for guidance and for the courage to do the things that need to be done? If so, then you're continually inviting your Creator to reveal Himself in a variety of ways. The result of regular communion with God is a closeness and a trust that empowers and encourages you to realign your values and commitments.

When we make God's priorities our priorities, we receive God's abundance and His peace. With God as our partner, we will walk calmly and confidently down the paths of His choosing. As we spend time in Scripture and prayer, our values start to shift: faithfulness overrides worldly success, busyness gives way to purpose, and self-promotion is replaced by service. God's priorities often look upside down to the world: loving our enemies, putting others first, and trusting Him over our judgment. But when we align our daily choices with His kingdom values, we begin to live with deeper peace and clarity.

Thinking Positive Thoughts

When you allow God to reign over your heart, He will honor you with spiritual blessings that are simply too numerous to count. So, as you plan for the day ahead, make God's will your ultimate priority. When you do, every other priority will tend to fall neatly into place.

Remember This

Even Jesus Himself prayed to the Father, "I want your will to be done, not mine" (Luke 22:42 NLT). To become like Jesus, open your hand and release everything of this earth you've been clinging to. Once your hand is empty, you can only imagine how God will choose to fill it!

How important it is for us—young and old—to live as if Jesus would return any day—to set our goals, make our choices, raise our children, and conduct business with the perspective of the imminent return of our Lord.

GLORIA GAITHER

22

Serving from the Inside Out

Be strong and courageous, and do the work. Don't be afraid or discouraged, for the LORD God, my God, is with you. He will not fail you or forsake you.

1 CHRONICLES 28:20 NLT

Jesus teaches that the most esteemed women are not the self-congratulatory leaders of society but rather the humblest of servants. But our human nature, or tendency, is not to serve. By nature, we seek to puff ourselves up, take what's "ours," and glorify our own accomplishments.

If ever anyone had reason to boast or brag, it would've been Jesus. Yet Jesus—the Son of God Himself—served others with humility, compassion, and love. He chose to spend His time on earth washing His disciples' feet, touching the untouchable, feeding the hungry, and caring for the brokenhearted. His example ought to remind us that serving our neighbors quietly and without commotion is more in alignment with God's will for us.

As a humble servant, you will glorify God. After all, earthly glory is fleeting—here today and gone all too soon. But heavenly glory endures throughout eternity. True greatness, Jesus proved, is found in serving others with a heart surrendered to God—in living a life of eternal impact.

Thinking Positive Thoughts

The contents of your thoughts, the direction of your steps, and the quality of your life will be determined, to a surprising extent, by the level of your service. God wants you to serve Him now, not later. What acts of service are on your heart that you can perform for Him today?

Remember This

Jesus Himself said, "For even the Son of Man came not to be served but to serve others and to give his life as a ransom for many" (Matthew 20:28 NLT). Reflect upon the good works that have been done for you by selfless and generous people—then follow in their footsteps by devoting yourself to kindness.

Serving others isn't about checking tasks off a list; it's about allowing the Holy Spirit to work in and through us to make an eternal impact.

Liz Curtis Higgs

23

Believing in Miracles

You are the God of great wonders! You demonstrate your awesome power among the nations.
Psalm 77:14 NLT

If you haven't noticed any of God's miracles lately, I would encourage you to look a bit closer! Throughout history, the Creator has intervened in the course of human events in ways that cannot be explained by science or human rationale. And He's still doing so today.

Reader's Digest recently asked readers to submit their examples of real-life, everyday miracles. One woman wrote in about her son surviving a horrific fall without even breaking a bone. Another woman described a near-death experience, and another expressed gratitude for being reunited with the daughter she'd long ago given up for adoption. The readers found hints of the miraculous in everything from a bumblebee in flight to the births of their children and grandchildren. One woman even found forgiveness to be an incredible, unlikely act.

God's miracles are not limited to special occasions, nor are they witnessed by a select few. God is crafting His wonders all around us: the miracle of lives transformed by God's love, mercy, and grace. Each day, God's magnificence is evident for all to see and experience. What have you seen today that you would consider a miracle of God?

Today seize the opportunity to inspect God's handiwork. Keep your eyes and your heart open. Be watchful, and you'll soon be amazed.

Thinking Positive Thoughts

Dwell for a moment on the truth that God has infinite power

and creativity. What beautiful things has He placed in your path today? What can you learn about God from His miracles, both large and small?

Remember This

When was the last time you asked God for a miracle? God is in the business of miraculous things—so don't be afraid to ask Him to do for you what He does best!

Be bold in your requests to God and hold out for miracles. He's brought me out of places I thought I would never escape, and He can do the same for you.

Tasha Layton

24

Distrusting Distorted Messages

Do not love this world nor the things it offers you, for when you love the world, you do not have the love of the Father in you.

1 John 2:15 NLT

Being a woman of faith can be hard, especially when the world keeps sending messages that are contrary to God's truth.

The culture around us wants to rearrange our priorities. We learn from social media ads and entertainment that appearance and social standing are all-important. Power, wealth, achievement, and other superficial standards are exalted, while kindness, generosity, and humility are rarely rewarded virtues.

As Christians, we know the important things in life have little to do with appearances, power, or popularity. Our faith in God, our families, our communities, and our eternal futures matter the most. *Period.*

God loves—our beauty, our skills, and our wealth have nothing to do with His enduring love. God's love is not built on these things. The next time you are feeling the pressure to be someone different from who you are, remember that your identity is in Christ—not in what the world says but in who God says you are: loved, chosen, and enough.

Thinking Positive Thoughts

The noise of the world has a way of attacking your thoughts, your senses, and your heart. So if you're serious about thinking more positively, pay attention instead to the voices and sounds that fill you with optimism and joy.

Remember This

The world around us may promote external beauty, success, and self-fulfillment as the highest goals, making many women feel inadequate if they don't match these superficial standards. But being a woman of God means clinging to the values of humility, kindness, and sacrificial love—values that lead to true satisfaction and joy.

God's plans don't look like the world's definition of success, but they always include lasting, eternal purpose and value. They also include His presence.

Helen Smallbone

25

Forgiving and Moving On from Difficult People

But the wisdom from above is first of all pure. It is also peace loving, gentle at all times, and willing to yield to others. It is full of mercy and the fruit of good deeds. It shows no favoritism and is always sincere.

James 3:17 NLT

People can be rude and cruel. They can be unfair, unkind, and unappreciative. Sometimes people get angry and frustrated. So what's a Christian to do?

God's answer is straightforward: Forgive, forget, and move on. In Luke 6:37, Jesus instructs, "Do not judge, and you will not be judged. Do not condemn, and you will not be condemned. Forgive, and you will be forgiven" (HCSB). His command advises us how to respond to unkindness, while gently reminding us that neither are we perfect people. We are to forgive transgressions because we ourselves have been forgiven. Jesus already paid the price.

Today and every day, try to cultivate a spirit of forgiveness. If you find yourself dwelling on the shortcomings of others, remind yourself that they, too, were created by God. And when other people misbehave (as they most certainly will from time to time), try not to take it personally. Say a prayer for them, say a prayer for yourself, and endeavor to move on as quickly as you can. Don't let the offense live rent-free in your head. You have better things to do!

Thinking Positive Thoughts

Try to remember the last time you acted poorly toward someone.

Did you have your reasons for your behavior? Are you sorry for it now? Keep that feeling at the front of your mind so you can show grace to the next person who offends or frustrates you. Everyone needs forgiveness—including you and me.

Remember This

Make room in your heart for forgiveness by releasing the things over which you have no control. Guard your words and your thoughts accordingly and enjoy the peace that comes from letting go.

When something robs you of your peace of mind, ask yourself if it is worth the energy you are expending on it. If not, then put it out of your mind in an act of discipline. Every time the thought of "it" returns, refuse it.

Kay Arthur

26

Saying No to Envy

A peaceful heart leads to a healthy body;
jealousy is like cancer in the bones.

PROVERBS 14:30 NLT

God's Word warns us about a dangerous, destructive state of mind: envy. Envy is emotional poison. It poisons the mind, hardens the heart, and blinds us to the blessings before us.

If we are to experience the abundant lives that Christ has promised, we must be on guard against envious thoughts. Jealousy breeds discontent, discontent breeds unhappiness, and unhappiness robs us of the peace that might otherwise be ours. The beast of jealousy also has no natural limit; it feeds on what others have without ever being satisfied.

If envy has invaded your heart and begun impacting your everyday attitude and choices, ask God to help you heal and find perspective. When you ask sincerely and often, He will respond by providing the peace that can only be found through Him. Rest in the comfort of knowing you have all you could possibly need in Jesus Christ.

Thinking Positive Thoughts

The best way to combat envy is with gratitude. When we are able to count our blessings and focus on what we already have, we feel contentment rather than empty longing. So choose thankfulness over striving!

Remember This

Have you ever heard the expression "Envy is the thief of joy"? In short, it means "Don't rob yourself of what you already have." Refuse to let feelings of envy invade your thoughts or your heart, choosing instead to count the many unique gifts God has already granted you.

The grass is always greener where you water it.
Instead of envying others,
nurture what God has given you.

Christine Caine

27

Acknowledging Your Adversary

So humble yourselves before God. Resist the devil, and he will flee from you.

James 4:7 NLT

This world is God's creation, and it contains the wonderful fruits of His handiwork. But the fallen world also holds countless opportunities to stray from God's will. Temptations are everywhere, and the devil, it seems, never takes a day off. As believers, our goal is to turn away from temptation and to place our lives squarely in the center of God's will. It's not easy, but it is what we are called to do.

In his letter to Jewish Christians, Peter offered a stern warning: "Be alert and of sober mind. Your enemy the devil prowls around like a roaring lion looking for someone to devour" (1 Peter 5:8 NIV). While some would like to pretend the devil is a fiction or a cartoonish character, what was true in New Testament times is equally true in our own. Evil abounds in the world, and our enemy continues to sow the seeds of destruction far and wide.

But we have no need to fear, for we are on the side of righteousness. Romans 16:20 assures us: "The God of peace will soon crush Satan under your feet" (NLT). To guard our hearts and face the foe before us, let us earnestly wrap ourselves in the powerful protection of God's holy Word.

Thinking Positive Thoughts

Evil exists. To pretend the enemy isn't real is to deny the danger he poses. Yet we are already victorious through Christ (Romans

8:37)! When faced with any sort of temptation, we can use the power granted us to run in the opposite direction.

Remember This

Evil does exist, and you will confront it. Prepare yourself by forming a genuine, life-changing relationship with God and His only begotten Son. There is darkness in this world, but take heart: God's light can overpower any darkness.

One of the biggest lies of the enemy is that we are not qualified to do God's work. May you find inner strength in this season to do everything God has called you to do!

CeCe Winans

28

Recharging Your Batteries

Be joyful. Grow to maturity. Encourage each other.
Live in harmony and peace. Then the
God of love and peace will be with you.

2 Corinthians 13:11 NLT

Even the most faithful woman can find herself running on empty. After all, she has a lot to do! Getting to work on time, running the carpool, figuring out where dinner will come from, making doctor's appointments, volunteering for church events—sometimes all before lunchtime on Monday!

The demands of daily life can drain us of our strength (and sanity!). But even more, the daily grind can rob us of the joy that is rightfully ours in Christ. When we find ourselves tired, discouraged, anxious, or worse, there is a Source from which we can draw the power needed to recharge our spiritual batteries. That source is our Father God. When we are weak or worried, He can heal our hearts.

Are you so tired you can barely sit up straight? Let your eyes close for a moment. Then turn your heart toward God. Take a moment of stillness for yourself and find some wordless communion with the Father. You don't even need to speak as you turn your thoughts toward Him; He already knows exactly what you need. As you take a few deep, calming breaths, try to relax into the silence. Your to-do list can wait as you steal these moments of peace and quiet throughout your day. The Creator of the universe stands waiting and ready, always able to create a new sense of wonderment and joy in you.

Thinking Positive Thoughts

God can make all things new, including you. Meditate upon a Scripture you love or repeat a prayer you know by heart. Your small moments with God don't have to be complicated to be full of rejuvenating calm.

Remember This

God wants to give you peace, and He wants to restore your spirit. If you're feeling weak or worried, spend time in His healing presence. He longs to have these moments with you.

In those desperate times when we feel like we don't have an ounce of strength, He will gently pick up our heads so that our eyes can behold something—something that will keep His hope alive in us.

Kathy Troccoli

29

Relying on an Unchanging God

For everything there is a season,
a time for every activity under heaven.
ECCLESIASTES 3:1 NLT

Our world is in a state of constant turmoil—yet our God is not. When the world seems to be trembling beneath our feet, we feel incapable of reckoning with the chaos. But we can be comforted in the knowledge that our heavenly Father is the rock that cannot be shaken. His Word promises, "I am the LORD, I do not change" (Malachi 3:6 NKJV). What joy it is to know our Creator is steadfast, solid, and secure! He never changes!

We encounter a multitude of changes—some good, some not so good. And on occasion, we have to endure life-changing personal losses that leave us breathless. When we do, our loving heavenly Father stands ready to protect us, to comfort us, to guide us and, in time, to heal us.

Are you facing difficult circumstances or unwelcome changes? Do you spend each day feeling burdened by the weight of an unpredictable future? If so, please remember that God is far bigger than any problem you may face. He already knows the future, and it is precisely because the Lord does not change that you can face whatever happens with courage.

Thinking Positive Thoughts

Today keep this thought in mind: Change is inevitable, but growth is not. Throughout your life, God will arrive at your doorstep with many opportunities to learn and to grow. Each time He knocks, your challenge, of course, is to open the door and answer.

Remember This

God remains steadfast. His character doesn't evolve, His promises don't expire, and His love doesn't waver based on our performance. So if a big change is called for, don't be afraid to make it. With God, one big leap is better than a thousand baby steps.

The only way to keep your balance is to fix your eyes on the One who never changes. If you gaze too long at your circumstances, you will become dizzy and confused.

SARAH YOUNG

30

Knowing When to Say No

Therefore, since we are surrounded by such a huge crowd of witnesses to the life of faith, let us strip off every weight that slows us down, especially the sin that so easily trips us up. And let us run with endurance the race God has set before us.

HEBREWS 12:1 NLT

If you haven't yet learned to say no—to say it politely, firmly, and often—you are likely inviting untold stress into your life. Why? Because if you can't say no (when appropriate) to family members, friends, or coworkers, you'll find yourself overcommitted and underappreciated.

Some of us who have trouble standing up for ourselves are afraid of being rejected. If that's the case for you, here's a reminder: Jesus was rejected too, and He *always* did the right thing, for the right reasons. If your willingness to please is interfering with your own good judgment or what you know to be God's priorities, you are likely standing in the way of the best plans God has for you. Don't be your own worst enemy by filling up your time with commitments that take away from the purposes of God.

If this message resonates with you, stand in front of a mirror and practice saying no. Kindly and courteously practice saying, "I'm sorry, but I can't." Rehearse your responses so when it's time to use them, you have them at the ready. Just know the world won't end if you disappoint someone—especially if the end result is protecting time and energy that can to belong to God.

Thinking Positive Thoughts

You have the right to say no to requests you consider unreasonable, irrelevant, or inconvenient. Don't feel guilty for asserting your right to say no, and don't feel compelled to fabricate excuses for your decisions. And remember: Saying no to the wrong things provides the opportunity to say yes to the right ones.

Remember This

The next time you are struggling to say no to something you know is wrong for you, imagine how your life would feel if you weren't overworked, overstressed, and undervalued. Ask God to help clarify your priorities if you need this specific direction. If your conscience says no, listen to its urging.

Let's face it. None of us can do a thousand things to the glory of God. And, in our own vain attempt to do so, we stand the risk of forfeiting a precious thing.

BETH MOORE

31

Sharing Your Faith with Boldness

Everyone who acknowledges me publicly here on earth, I will also acknowledge before my Father in heaven.

MATTHEW 10:32 NLT

Genuine, heartfelt Christianity can be highly contagious. When we've experienced the transforming power of God's love, we feel the need to share the Good News of His only begotten Son. Through words and actions, we share our testimony—though not necessarily in that order.

Every believer, including you, bears responsibility for sharing God's Good News. After His resurrection and before His ascension, Jesus commissioned us by saying, "Go and make disciples of all the nations, baptizing them in the name of the Father and the Son and the Holy Spirit" (Matthew 28:19 NLT). Though God is omnipotent and does not need our assistance, how wonderful it is that He has included us in His plan to bring about His eternal kingdom!

Today don't be bashful or timid; talk about Jesus and show the world what it really means to follow Him. After all, the fields are ripe for the harvest, time is short, and the workers are surprisingly few. Your role in building the kingdom is a crucial one—and the people who meet Jesus because of you will never forget the part you played in God's story.

Thinking Positive Thoughts

When it comes to expanding the kingdom of God, you have a profound responsibility to the people around you. Your silence isn't optional, so if you are trying to muster the right words to say, start with the simple, straightforward truth about your faith story. A script or a formula may fall flat, but an earnest word about Jesus will do wonders in comparison.

Remember This

If you have allowed Christ to reign over your heart, you have an important story to tell: *yours.* Your testimony doesn't have to be flashy or miraculous; let the simple truth of your story sway hearts in God's direction, and He will manage the rest.

God taught me a lesson. He said,
"If you just obey me, I know how to touch every heart."
CeCe Winans

32

Taking in More of God's Word

You will be a good servant of Christ Jesus, nourished by the words of the faith and the good teaching that you have followed.

1 Timothy 4:6 HCSB

God's Word is unlike any other book you've read. Sixty-six books penned by multiple writers over the course of thousands of years, the Bible is a roadmap for life here on earth and for life into eternity.

As Christians, we are called to study the Bible, to trust its promises, to follow its commandments, and to share its Good News with the world. Yet when we treat studying God's Word as yet another item on our never-ending to-do lists, we lose sight of the fact that reading God's Word is a wonderful means by which we grow closer to our Father.

If you find the idea of studying the Bible tiring or intimidating, try to reframe the task as an opportunity for quiet meditation. To be able to read the Word of God is a privilege—not a chore—and to forfeit the chance to read Scripture is to deprive ourselves of a closer relationship to our Creator. God's holy Word is a transforming, life-changing, one-of-a-kind treasure. And the more you get to know God's Word, the more you will also understand His will.

Thinking Positive Thoughts

Look for creative ways to take in God's words each day, such as phone apps, audiobooks, or online women's groups that share and study Scripture a little at a time. Choose a verse or two to memorize. Then dwell on those verses until they are seared into your heart and mind. Guided journals and other workbooks can lead to fruitful study as well.

Remember This

Even if you've been studying the Bible for many years, you still have plenty to learn. Though Scripture doesn't change, you and I do—meaning we bring new insight and experience to the steadfast Word of God each time we revisit it.

Take time for the Word. Take time to read.
Ask Him after you're done reading it,
"What are You trying to show me, Lord,
through this? How is this a part of my story?"

JACI VELASQUEZ

33

Listening Carefully to the Creator

Anyone who belongs to God listens gladly to the words of God.

JOHN 8:47 NLT

As you search for solutions to the inevitable challenges of everyday life, keep the lines of communication open with your heavenly Father. And after you've finished talking, listen carefully for His reply.

God has always spoken to His people in different ways. In the Bible, we read about God speaking to Moses through a burning bush (Exodus 3). He communicated with Daniel through a vision (Daniel 2). He often spoke through prophets, as well as angels and other messengers. And that was only in the Old Testament!

Sometimes God speaks loudly and clearly. But more often, He speaks in a still, small voice that's best heard in silence. Carving out quiet moments each day to pray, meditate, or study His Word can aid us as we endeavor to interpret His direction.

Are you ready to pray sincerely and to wait patiently for God's response? And are you attuned to the subtle guidance of your intuition? If you sincerely desire to hear His voice and discern His will for you, make time today to listen carefully. A quiet, willing heart will certainly receive His intended message.

Thinking Positive Thoughts

Prayer is two-way communication with God, but it doesn't have to be a formal thing. Talking to God throughout your day and requesting His input on the smallest questions can "count" as prayer and communion too. It can be an ongoing conversation like you have with a friend.

Remember This

If you're having trouble hearing God, slow down and do your best to tune out the distractions. Sometimes God will shout over the noise of our lives, but we must also be willing to listen.

If we want to hear from the Lord, we must confess that sometimes we walk right past the Lord's instruction and set ourselves up to miss His direction. If we want His direction for our decisions, the great cravings of our souls must not only be the big moments of assignment. They must also be the seemingly small instructions in the most ordinary of moments.

Lysa TerKeurst

34

Focusing on Joy

Look straight ahead, and fix your eyes on what lies before you.

Proverbs 4:25 NLT

This day—and every day hereafter—is a chance to celebrate the life God has given you. It's also a chance to give thanks to the One who has offered you more blessings than you can possibly count. Is that what you are focusing on today? Are you channeling your energy toward God's blessings and His wonderful will for your life?

Erasing negative thoughts from our minds would be impossible. Bad things happen, and we aren't expected to ignore them. But with God's gifts at the front of our minds, we are less likely to sink into the mire of negativity. Good outcomes seem more likely, and opportunities seem more fortuitous. When we meditate on our reasons for joy, our reasons for feeling doubt and despair simply can't compete any longer.

Today why not focus your thoughts on the joy that is rightfully yours in Christ? Why not take time to celebrate God's glorious creation? Why not invest in your hopes instead of your fears? When you do, your world will seem brighter, and you can then share your optimism with others. To be a bearer of joy and light for the sake of our wonderful Creator is a fantastic appointment indeed.

Thinking Positive Thoughts

Think about all your current commitments, especially the ones taking up large blocks of your time. Then rank those activities in order of their importance. Is the least important activity on your list encouraging joy or discouragement in your heart? If this commitment is not furthering God's kingdom or leading you down the path of joy, could you possibly let go of this obligation or task?

Remember This

When we focus on what matters most—starting with God's blessings and promises—the quality of our lives will improve. We won't be distracted by past setbacks and future what-ifs. Instead, we will find joy in the present moment.

Measure the size of the obstacles against the size of God.

Beth Moore

35

Celebrating the Small Things

Try to please them all the time, not just when they are watching you. As slaves of Christ, do the will of God with all your heart. Work with enthusiasm, as though you were working for the Lord rather than for people.

EPHESIANS 6:6–7 NLT

Today, like every other, is a priceless gift from God. He has offered us another opportunity to serve Him with smiling faces and willing hands. When we do our part, He inevitably does His part—provides us with more joy than we can imagine.

If you'd like to worry less, try celebrating more. If you really think about it, celebrating shouldn't be very hard if you believe each day holds its own share of blessings. A good hair day, a delicious meal, and a weekly paycheck are all good reasons for a high five. Congratulate yourself for figuring out the daily crossword. Pat yourself on the back for paying a bill on time. No win is too small, no achievement too insignificant. They are all signs that God is still taking care of us.

The Lord has promised to bless you and keep you, now and forever—so don't wait for birthdays or holidays to celebrate. Make this day an exciting adventure. And while you're at it, take time to thank the Lord for it all. He deserves your sincere gratitude, and expressing your thanks will also bring you joy.

Thinking Positive Thoughts

As a believer, you have many reasons to be enthusiastic about your life, your faith, and your future. So don't wait for enthusiasm to find you; go looking for it.

Remember This

When you become genuinely enthused about your life, your faith, and your future, you'll begin seeing the silver linings and missing the rainclouds altogether.

It's the little things—like a sunrise, a kind gesture, or a moment of quiet—that remind us to celebrate God's presence in our daily lives.

MANDISA

36

Slowing Down

Be careful not to forget the Lord.

Deuteronomy 6:12 NLT

In a world that constantly demands more—more projects, more achieving, more busyness—it's easy to lose sight of the gentle invitation from God to simply *be*. For women juggling responsibilities, relationships, and expectations, slowing down can feel like a luxury. But in God's presence, rest is not a reward; it's a calling.

Psalm 46:10 says, "Be still, and know that I am God!" (NLT). Stillness isn't weakness; it's trusting that God will keep things going while we pause. When we slow down, we make space for God to remind us who He is and who we are in Him. You don't have to earn His love or prove your worth. He delights in you simply because you're His.

Has the busy pace of life robbed you of the peace and contentment you believe are rightfully yours? Do you have too many obligations and too few hours in which to get them done? If so, remember that God is in control. You have permission to slow down and let Him handle the rest. Today, as a gift to yourself, to your family, and to the world, slow down, take a deep breath, and claim the inner peace that is your spiritual birthright: the peace of Jesus Christ. His peace, like His love, is offered freely.

Thinking Positive Thoughts

The Christian life isn't about checking boxes or doing more. It's about breathing deep, opening your heart, and letting God's peace fill the empty spaces. Look for His comfort amid quiet mornings, whispered prayers, a walk outside, or a moment of gratitude. Give Him room to do His best work through your stillness.

Remember This

God wants you to experience peace, and He wants you to have time for quiet reflection and prayer. The world, on the other hand, wants to steal your attention and gobble up your time. When in doubt, trust God. His tranquil presence will calm your soul.

"Slowing down doesn't mean we're lazy or unproductive; it means we're choosing to prioritize our relationship with God and the things that truly matter."

JENNIE ALLEN

37

Sharing God's Love

Dear friends, since God loved us that much, we surely ought to love each other.

1 John 4:11 NLT

Sometimes, amid the crush of everyday life, God may seem very far away. However, He *is* never far away! The Lord is always with us, night and day. He never leaves us, even for a moment.

God loves us so much that He sent His only Son, Jesus Christ, to die for you and me. Now, because we are wondrous creations treasured by God, a question presents itself: What will we do in response to God's love? Will we treasure it? Will we share it? Will we take this perfect gift for granted?

When you embrace God's love, you are transformed. When you embrace God's love, you feel differently about yourself, your neighbors, and your world. When you embrace God's love, you can keep your problems in perspective because you know that every earthly inconvenience is temporary but that God's love is eternal.

We express our gratitude for Christ's great sacrifice when we share the message of God's grace with others. Not only can sharing the gospel change eternity for the people we meet; it also demonstrates to the Father that we are thankful for what He's done for us. Let's not store up the inexhaustible Good News of Jesus for ourselves. There is enough salvation to go around!

Thinking Positive Thoughts

When you choose to focus your thoughts on God's love for you, you'll find it easier to share His love with others. In fact, you'll find it hard to keep the gospel to yourself!

Remember This

The next time you feel discouraged or afraid, remember this: When all else fails, God's love does not. You can always depend upon His love, and His grace extends to each person who chooses to accept it.

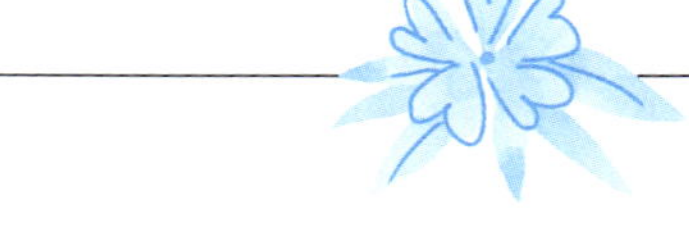

God wants to reveal Himself as your heavenly Father. When you are hurting, you can run to Him and crawl up into His lap. When you wonder which way to turn, you can grasp His strong hand, and He'll guide you along life's path. When everything around you is falling apart, you'll feel your Father's arm around your shoulder to hold you together.

Lisa Whelchel

38

Taking Your Doubts to God

If you need wisdom, ask our generous God, and he will give it to you. He will not rebuke you for asking. But when you ask him, be sure that your faith is in God alone. Do not waver, for a person with divided loyalty is as unsettled as a wave of the sea that is blown and tossed by the wind.

JAMES 1:5–6 NLT

Even some of the most faithful Christians, at times, are faced with occasional bouts of discouragement and doubt. But even when we feel far removed from God, God is never far removed from us. He is always with us, always willing to calm the storms of life, always willing to replace our doubts with comfort and assurance.

Whenever you're plagued by doubts, your inclination may be to remove yourself further from your faith walk. Concerned or ashamed that your doubts may be visible to all, perhaps you've avoided going to church, reading the Word, or spending time with your Christian community. Even so, that's precisely the moment you should seek God's presence the most. Open your heart to Him, expressing your fears and questions. He already knows your thoughts and worries, so acknowledging them is more about admitting them to yourself. Be assured that in time, God will calm your fears, answer your prayers, and restore your confidence once again. No question or doubt in your mind is too big for our wondrous, all-knowing Father.

Thinking Positive Thoughts

Do not be afraid to name your doubts and lay them before the Father. You will never regret genuinely seeking to establish a deeper, more meaningful relationship with Him—and He will never let you linger in the pit of despair and disbelief.

Remember This

God responds to our doubts with patience, compassion, and truth. He doesn't shame us for wrestling with questions; rather, He invites us to bring them to Him.

I felt the Lord would give me the strength to endure whatever I had to face. God did away with all my fear.

Rosa Parks

39

Avoiding the Trap of Perfectionism

If you wait for perfect conditions, you will never get anything done.

ECCLESIASTES 11:4 TLB

Expectations, expectations, expectations! As a woman living in the twenty-first century, you know that demands can be high, and expectations even higher. Entertainment, social media, and other channels deliver an endless stream of messages that tell you how to look, how to behave, how to eat, and how to dress. Some expectations are impossible to meet—but the good news is, God's expectations are not.

God doesn't expect you to be perfect. In fact, the reason He sent His Son to earth was because He already knew we would all fall short of perfection. But that doesn't mean God doesn't have *any* expectations of us. His Word is full of advice for living and commandments about loving Him and others. Everything else is inconsequential and arbitrary by comparison.

So do your best to please God and don't worry too much about what other people think. Their impossible standards are ever-changing, and most of them can't be pleased anyway. Focus your efforts instead on the One who wants the best for you. His yoke is easy, and His burden is light (Matthew 11:30).

Thinking Positive Thoughts

If you are feeling inadequate, "less than", or insecure today, remember that God doesn't expect or even want perfection; He only wants your heart. His love has no conditions, and nothing in heaven or on earth can ever separate you from the love of Christ (Romans 8:38–39)!

Remember This

In heaven, we will know perfection. Here on earth, we have a few short years to wrestle with the challenges of imperfection. God is perfect; we humans are not—and that is okay. May we live, love, and forgive accordingly.

God is so inconceivably good. He's not looking for perfection. He already saw it in Christ. He's looking for affection.

BETH MOORE

40

Stewarding God's Gifts

God has given each of you a gift
from his great variety of spiritual gifts.
Use them well to serve one another.

1 Peter 4:10 NLT

The spiritual gifts of God are special abilities given by the Holy Spirit to believers for the purpose of building up the church and glorifying God. They are not earned or self-generated; they are blessings meant to be used in love and service—and each of God's daughters has received such gifts from the Father.

Not every believer has the same gift, but every believer has *been gifted.* These individual strengths are meant to work together like parts of a body—unique and diverse yet united in purpose (1 Corinthians 12:12–27). Together, as believers, we are called to make use of the giftings bestowed upon us by God.

Have you discovered the gifts you possess? If so, remember they are meant to be shared. Everyone has giftings or talents that are specific to them. Hone your gifts and use them for God's glory. All your talents, opportunities, and giftings are on temporary loan from the Creator. Use them while you can because time is short and the needs are great. Then, just as He promised, the Lord will bless you now and forever.

Thinking Positive Thoughts

If you are unsure what your spiritual gifts are, don't hesitate to ask a friend or two! Often the people closest to us are better able to recognize our strengths than we are.

Armed with feedback from your friends, make a list of your skills and abilities. Include everything you do well, no matter how seemingly small or significant. Spend some time praying over your list, asking God to make the most of what He's given you. God can make use of *everything*—so don't be surprised when He does!

Remember This

God has given you a unique array of talents, tools, and opportunities, and He desires for you to be a faithful steward of those treasures. As you use His gifts wisely, also prepare yourself for the blessings that are sure to follow.

The great thing about our God is that
He does not call people who are already equipped.
He calls you—and then for the people that
say yes, He equips them with what they need.

Priscilla Shirer

41

Making Peace with the Past

Do not remember the past events, pay no attention to things of old. Look, I am about to do something new; even now it is coming. Do you not see it? Indeed, I will make a way in the wilderness, rivers in the desert.

ISAIAH 43:18–19 HCSB

Since we can't change the pains and disappointments of the past, why do so many of us tend to replay them over and over again in our minds? Perhaps it's because we can't find it in our hearts to forgive the people who have hurt us. Being mere mortals, we seek revenge, not reconciliation, and we harbor hatred in our hearts, sometimes for decades. Or perhaps we struggle to forgive ourselves for weakness and failures. We revisit our errors and imagine how things might've turned out differently. Whatever the case, we cannot change the past.

The present, of course, is a different matter. Today is filled with opportunities to live, to love, to work, to play, and to celebrate life. If we sincerely wish to build a better tomorrow, we can start building it today, in the present moment.

If you've endured a difficult past, ask God to help you accept it. Try to be grateful for what you've learned from it. Ask for divine help to forgive those involved, including yourself. Then the next time you find your thoughts lingering there, do your best to reroute your thinking toward the present—a place and time where opportunities abound and change is still possible.

Thinking Positive Thoughts

The past cannot be changed, no matter how often we think about it. If you find yourself investing your emotional energy in something that happened long ago, try writing about the experience in a journal or notebook. Write again and again about what happened until you feel like a broken record. Sometimes writing leads to breakthroughs and healing as we process our thoughts and discover how far we've already come. Other times, you may grow so bored with your hang-up that you decide it's no longer worth your time, paper, and ink.

Remember This

You can't build a better tomorrow if you're spending all your time thinking about yesterday.

Take what you can from an experience. Then endeavor to apply those lessons to the future. With God, nothing is wasted—not even our biggest mistakes!

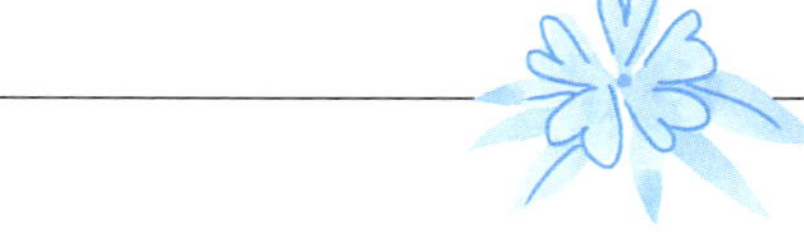

Let go of your past! Let go of what you can't control—and rest in the knowledge that God is in control!

Sheila Walsh

42

Dreaming Big Dreams

Now glory be to God, who by his mighty power at work within us is able to do far more than we would ever dare to ask or even dream.

EPHESIANS 3:20 TLB

Are you willing to entertain the possibility that God has big plans in store for you?

Your heavenly Father created you with unique gifts and untapped talents. Your job, today, is to tap into them. When you do, you'll begin to feel an increasing sense of confidence in yourself and in your future.

Dreaming big dreams with God means opening your heart to His limitless possibilities—not just pursuing your own plans but surrendering your imagination, goals, and gifts to His purpose. To dream with God means believing He can do more than our imaginations could conceive of and having the faith to step into goals that may feel too big, too scary, or too uncertain without Him.

It takes courage to dream big dreams. You will discover that courage when you do three things: accept the past, trust God to handle the future, and make the most of the time He has given you today.

Nothing is too difficult for God, and no dreams are too big for Him—not even yours. So start living—and dreaming—accordingly.

Thinking Positive Thoughts

Your attitude toward the future will define and direct your course. So think realistically about yourself and your situation but focus your thoughts on hopes, not fears. When you are in doubt about pursuing something big, ask yourself: "Who am I to stand in God's way?" (Acts 11:17). When His will is part of the dream, nothing is impossible.

Remember This

You can dream big dreams, but you can never out-dream God. His plans for you are bigger, wilder, and more thrilling than anything you can imagine for yourself.

Your dreams are worth fighting for,
and while you're not in control
of all the variables, you can be in charge
of your character, choices, and creativity.

ANN VOSKAMP

43

Asking God for the Things You Need

Ask, and it will be given to you; seek, and you will find; knock, and it will be opened to you. For everyone who asks receives, and he who seeks finds, and to him who knocks it will be opened.

Matthew 7:7–8 NKJV

God invites us to ask Him for the things we need, and He promises to hear our prayers as well as our thoughts. The Lord is always available, and He's always ready to help us. And He knows precisely what we need—but He still instructs us to ask.

Do you make a habit of asking God for the things you need? The idea of asking for something may seem simple, but for some of us, acknowledging our need is hard. To admit we want or require help may wound our pride or damage our perceived self-sufficiency, but being a child of God involves confessing our flaws, shortcomings, and sin.

He can do great things through us if we have the courage to ask for His guidance and His help. So be fervent in prayer and don't hesitate to ask the Creator for the tools you need to accomplish His plan for your life. Then get busy and expect the best. When you do your part, God will most certainly do His part. Great things are bound to happen.

Thinking Positive Thoughts

The Lord wants to hear from you anytime you have a need. Here's a short prayer you can use to welcome His divine assistance:

Dear God,

I come to You today with a need on my heart. You know my situation better than I do, and I trust that You care. I ask for [fill in the blank], and I pray for Your will to be done above all. Thank You for hearing me and for always being near.

In Your Son's name,

Amen

Remember This

To live in God's will to the fullest, it's important to trust Him *and* to believe in yourself. The first step in accomplishing big things is to believe that you and God, working together, can accomplish big things.

If you feel completely in the dark, ask God to give you a flash of light. That is a prayer that He would love to answer.

Mandisa

44

Envisioning a Bright Future

"For I know the plans I have for you," says the Lord. "They are plans for good and not for disaster, to give you a future and a hope."

Jeremiah 29:11 NLT

When problems arise—as they often do—the future may seem foreboding. You may wonder if you can make it through one day, let alone the ones to come. But if you take your troubles to the Lord and leave them there, your future is secure.

Are you willing to place your future in the hands of a loving and all-knowing Creator? Do you trust in the ultimate goodness of His plan for you? Will you face today's challenges with hope and optimism? If you are wavering on your answers, take a moment to think about how far God has already carried you. Has He ever abandoned you, or has He kept His promises and already sustained you through the hardest times?

God created you for a very important purpose: *His* purpose. And you still have important work to do: *His* work. So today, as you live in the present and look to the future, remember that God has a marvelous plan for you. Trust His heart more than your own plans. He promises purpose, peace, and His presence in every one of your steps.

Thinking Positive Thoughts

Picture a life where you are living to the fullest in your divine calling—using your gifts to serve others, walking in freedom from your past, and growing deeper in your faith. What details can you add to this picture? Where are you, and who is surrounding you? How do you feel, and what are you doing each day? Meditate on this vision. Then take tiny steps toward making it reality through prayer *and* action.

Remember This

When you align your desires with your Father's will, He begins shaping your vision through prayer, Scripture, and the gentle nudges of the Holy Spirit. A future designed by God may not look exactly like your expectations—but it will always be filled with eternal meaning, and you will always be supported by His hand.

If know if God has called me to something that He already has the race marked out.

MADISON CAIN JOHNSON

45

Encouraging Your Family and Friends

May God, who gives this patience and encouragement, help you live in complete harmony with each other, as is fitting for followers of Christ Jesus.

Romans 15:5 NLT

Think about a woman in your life who is an encouragement to everyone she meets. What is her personality like? How does she use her words? How would you describe her spirit? How does her presence make most people feel?

One of the reasons God put us here is to serve and encourage others, starting with the people who live under our roof. But the opportunities for us to strengthen each other do not stop with our families. By using our words to build up instead of tear down, we can offer support to those in our church families, our workplaces, our communities, and beyond. And a benefit of encouraging others is that they often do the very same for us.

As a follower of the Lord, you have the opportunity to become a beacon of encouragement to the world. How can you do it? First, look for the good in others, and second, celebrate the good you find. As the old saying goes, "When someone does something good, applaud. You'll make two people happy!"

Even a brief word of appreciation can make a big difference in someone's life. So today, make a concerted effort to thank someone for their service. Pay a compliment to someone who deserves it. Take a page from the book of that woman you know who already encourages well. Soon, with enough practice, you may become the example of an encourager that others look to for inspiration.

Thinking Positive Thoughts

Encouragers need encouragement too! Take a little time today to reach out to someone who has supported you and helped you carry on, whether recently or long ago. Let them know that their words and efforts have not been in vain. Certainly, you will both be encouraged by such a moment of mutual appreciation.

Remember This

When you help other people feel better about themselves, you'll feel better about yourself too. Not to mention, hope and encouragement tend to trickle down in surprising ways—so why not be the one who opens the floodgate of kindness?

Kind words can be short and easy to speak, but their echoes are truly endless.

MOTHER TERESA

46

Counting Blessings, Not Complaints

Be hospitable to one another without complaining.
1 Peter 4:9 HCSB

Most of us have more blessings than we can count, yet we can still find reasons to complain about the minor frustrations of everyday life. Why do we do this? Whatever our reasons, to complain endlessly is not only shortsighted; it is also a serious roadblock on the path to spiritual abundance.

The inconveniences of life are inevitable. Even the best days feature flat tires, missed deadlines, runny noses, and burnt toast. But the thing about complaining is that it *rarely* does us any good. Complaining about minor setbacks doesn't prevent them or make them go away. Instead, dwelling on the things that annoy us only keeps those annoyances at the center of our thoughts.

By shifting our thoughts toward gratitude, we are choosing to ponder God's faithfulness instead. When we intentionally name our blessings—big or small—we train our hearts to trust God more and worry less. We no longer "sweat the small stuff," as they say. Rather, we look for the light that overcomes the darkness. Soon we will be unfazed by the annoyances that once took up so much of our time and emotional energy.

So the next time you're tempted to complain about the unavoidable hardships of everyday living, count your blessings instead. You will soon discover your heart is more fully at peace.

Thinking Positive Thoughts

Complaining focuses on what's wrong, what's missing, or what didn't go your way. It often feeds frustration, comparison, and discouragement. But when you choose to count your blessings, you begin to see how much God has already provided—even amid difficult seasons.

Remember This

Gratitude doesn't ignore hardship; it merely transforms how you endure it. Counting your blessings keeps your eyes on the Giver, not just the gifts. Choosing to be thankful makes room for joy, hope, and a healthy, renewed perspective.

Joy is the settled assurance that God is in control of all the details of my life, the quiet confidence that ultimately everything is going to be all right, and the determined choice to praise God in all things.

Kay Warren

47

Asking God for Answers

Don't worry about anything, but in everything, through prayer and petition with thanksgiving, let your requests be made known to God.

PHILIPPIANS 4:6 HCSB

Have you asked God for His guidance in every aspect of your life? If so, then you're continually inviting your Creator to reveal Himself in a variety of ways. Asking Him for answers is an act of worship, faith, and relationship—not just a process of seeking information, but of turning your heart toward Him with trust and humility.

Because communing with God was important, Jesus taught His disciples how to pray. He also modeled the process for them, even through the final moments of His earthly life. Genuine, heartfelt prayer produces powerful changes in us and in our world, and as disciples, we also have open lines of communication with the Father. When we lift our hearts to God in heaven, we open ourselves to a never-ending source of divine wisdom and infinite love.

Do you have questions about your future that you simply can't answer? Are you at a crossroads and in need of a road map? Ask for the guidance of your heavenly Father. Then continue asking Him for direction each day. Whatever your need, no matter how great or small, pray about it and never lose hope. God is not just near; He is here—and He's ready to listen to you right now.

Thinking Positive Thoughts

Though God already knows what you need in this life, try praying as specifically as possible. The act of articulating your questions, desires, and needs is more for your benefit than for God's.

At the same time, keep your mind open for how He will choose to respond. Be still, listen, and wait with patience. Sometimes His silence is part of the answer—leading you to trust, grow, or take a step of faith.

Remember This

If you have a big decision to make, be honest with God about your need for guidance. Ultimately, the goal is not just to get answers, but to grow closer to the One who holds them—and He will not withhold a good thing from His daughter (Matthew 7:9–11).

Prayer keeps us in constant communion with God, which is the goal of our entire believing lives.

Beth Moore

48

Letting God Be the Judge

Do not judge others, and you will not be judged. Do not condemn others, or it will all come back against you. Forgive others, and you will be forgiven.

Luke 6:37 NLT

The Bible instructs us to avoid judging others—yet even the most thoughtful among us may fall prey to the powerful yet subtle temptation to do so.

We often judge others because of insecurity, pride, or misunderstanding. But at its root, our judgment tends to come from a desire to elevate ourselves. When we compare, criticize, or look down on others, we can feel more in control, more righteous, or more secure—at least for a time. Ultimately, judging others is not a satisfying behavior. The act can fill our hearts with hateful, toxic feelings, and it can even lead to self-loathing.

As Jesus came upon a young woman who had been condemned by the Pharisees, He spoke not only to the crowd that was gathered there, but also to all generations when He warned, "He that is without sin among you, let him first cast a stone at her" (John 8:7 KJV). Christ divinely knew the hearts of the crowd, and He didn't like what He saw. His admonishment recognized an ugliness that is all too common in our weakness as humans.

None of us is immune to such posturing—but we are all in need of God's powerful grace. So the next time you're troubled by the temptation to judge another person, focus instead on your own need for redemption. Don't be a judge; be a witness to God's righteousness and overflowing mercy. That is God's better will for us.

Thinking Positive Thoughts

If you catch yourself being overly judgmental, try to remember that judgment can also be based on wrongheaded assumptions. We can never know another person's full story, yet we make conclusions based on appearance, behavior, or a moment in time. Without compassion or curiosity, we lose our way—so let us cling instead to the compassion Jesus has offered us and choose to cover others with the same gifts of mercy and grace.

Remember This

As believers, we have freely been given grace—a gift we did not earn, and a gift we do not deserve. May we never lose sight of the fact that despite our many imperfections, Jesus died so we might be considered holy enough to spend eternity with God.

Judging others is a heavy burden that we were never meant to carry. Release that weight and trust in God's perfect, righteous judgment.

Lisa Bevere

49

Battling Discouragement

We can rejoice, too, when we run into problems and trials, for we know that they help us develop endurance. And endurance develops strength of character, and character strengthens our confident hope of salvation.

Romans 5:3–4 NLT

All days are not created equal. Some days are bright and cheery, while other days are decidedly darker. When tough times inevitably arise, we are tempted to complain, to worry, and to do little else. A far better strategy, of course, is to pray more, to focus on the positives, and immerse ourselves in blessing others. But knowing what we *should* do and actually *doing* it are two separate things.

Sometimes even the most hopeful, optimistic, faith-filled women can become discouraged. But battling discouragement and trusting in God go hand in hand—because trust anchors the heart when everything else feels uncertain.

If you find yourself enduring difficult circumstances, try the following faith-filled steps:

First, *tell God exactly how you feel.* He isn't afraid of your sadness, doubts, or weariness. Pour it out in prayer, just as King David did in the Psalms.

Next, *remind yourself that God remains in heaven.* He is a God of possibility, not negativity, and His character is unchanging, faithful, loving, and near. What He's done before, He can do again. He has always come through for you.

Finally, *take one small step forward in faith.* Read one Bible verse, reach out to one mentor or church friend, listen to one hymn of praise, or encourage someone else. God sees and honors even the smallest of your efforts. Slowly but surely, your confidence will be restored.

Thinking Positive Thoughts

Sometimes our losses mean starting over—*from scratch*. When we encounter disappointments and tragedies of life, we do so with the ultimate armor: God's promises and equipping power. God's love will heal us if we cling to Him in our hearts. And the best time to cling to Him is right now, every day.

Remember This

Trusting God doesn't mean you'll never feel discouraged; it means coming back to Him whenever you do. Difficult days will come and go, but God's presence is never far away.

In times of discouragement,
lean into God's Word.
His truth can lift you above
the storm and restore your hope.

Priscilla Shirer

50

Being Still Before God

Be still, and know that I am God.
Psalm 46:10 NKJV

The world we live in is noisy, filled with distractions, frustrations, and complications. But when we allow the cacophony of a noisy world to separate us from God's peace, we do ourselves a profound disservice.

Brother Lawrence was a seventeenth-century monk who wrote a lot about prayer and meditation. While his life looked very different from that of a twenty-first-century woman's (he lived in a monastery), his advice could still be applied in ways that might be useful to Christians of today. His suggestions include:

- Praying and making time for God while doing chores
- Conversing with God in short spurts throughout the day
- Doing small things with great love

Do you tend to rush through the day with scarcely a single moment for quiet contemplation and prayer? If so, don't beat yourself up. Feeling guilty about your busyness won't do anything to change your heart or habits. Rather, gently take the moments that present themselves to you and try to spend them quietly with your Creator. Over time, the process of stilling or quietening your mind and heart with Him will become second nature.

Claim the inner peace of God that is your spiritual birthright. He offers it freely; it is yours for the asking. No moment of stillness with God is too small.

Thinking Positive Thoughts

Remember, the goal of spending time with the Father is not to "get something done." Don't think of it as a to-do list item at which you hope to excel. Rather, the goal is simply to *be* with Him—to still oneself and enjoy His presence. Yes, He has important things to share with you, but focus first on the joy that comes from His peace and calm.

Remember This

Carving out quiet time with God is less about escaping daily life and more about inviting God into it, moment by moment. We can't avoid all responsibilities, and we can't ignore life's demands—but we can learn to welcome God into our everyday tasks, and He will gladly join us when we do.

Time, like life, isn't about how much we have;
it's about what we do with it.

SARAH JAKES ROBERTS

51

Giving God Your Best

Wherever your treasure is,
there the desires of your heart will also be.
LUKE 12:34 NLT

Giving God your best isn't about perfection; it's about *devotion*. It's choosing to honor Him with your time, your talents, and your energy. As women, life often pulls us in many directions—family, work, responsibilities, relationships, and beyond. But God isn't asking for a flawless performance. He's simply inviting us to offer what we have with willing hearts.

Giving God your best might look like waking up early to pray, even when you're tired. It might mean using your creativity, special skills, or leadership to serve and love others well. It may be saying yes to a calling that feels bigger than you or saying no to something that distracts you from your time with Him. Whatever it is, your "best" is found in daily faithfulness, not grand gestures.

Does God abide over your heart? Honor Him by using the gifts He's given you to the fullest. God should come first, and that's the place He deserves in your heart.

Thinking Positive Thoughts

Because God is infinite and eternal, you cannot comprehend Him—but you can understand the desire to praise Him, love Him, and obey His Word. His incredible power and love for us compels a lifetime of heartfelt worship. We give Him our best not out of obligation, but because He first loved us (1 John 4:19).

Remember This

God sees every quiet act of love, every sacrifice no one else notices. When you give Him your best, even if it feels small, look for the ways He will inevitably multiply it.

We need to stand in awe of God and be blown away by His power. But His kindness and His love are really what draw us into a relationship with Him. His love makes us desire to know Him and to love Him in return.

Rebecca St. James

52

Seeking God Right Here, Right Now

The Lord is with you when you are with Him.
If you seek Him, He will be found by you.
2 Chronicles 15:2 HCSB

There's a reason why Scripture reminds us to pause and look for God. Perhaps for many thousands of years, people have been prone to distraction—as if it's human nature for us to get wrapped up in our various worldly endeavors. So when the psalmist reminds us to "Be still, and know that I am God," we can easily assume that many generations of busy, distracted people have benefited from this useful, straightforward command.

How do you most easily commune with the Creator? During worship service? As you're studying His Word? Perhaps you sense God in the wonders of nature or on the faces of children or in the majesty of a landscape. However you best experience the Father, try to cultivate such moments of stillness and devotion. When you dwell in the presence of your Creator's infinite love and power, He, in turn, will speak directly to your heart.

Be comforted in the knowledge that God is not just near; He is here alongside you, loving you, waiting for you to acknowledge Him. May each revelation bring you closer to His glorious Spirit.

Thinking Positive Thoughts

Sometimes you find God through a calmness that doesn't make sense, conviction that redirects you, or comfort amid your sorrow. If you are experiencing a kind of peace that defies worldly understanding (Philippians 4:7), it's safe to say the Holy Spirit may be gently nudging your heart.

Remember This

Sensing God isn't always dramatic; it's often quiet, simple, and deeply personal. If you have felt distant from the Father lately, ask Him to make you more aware. He loves to draw near.

A person won't realize the incredible magnitude of what God has in store for them until they are all-in in their relationship with Him.

HELEN SMALLBONE

53

Becoming a Disciple

The Lord *has told you what is good, and this is what he requires of you: to do what is right, to love mercy, and to walk humbly with your God..*

Micah 6:8 NLT

When Jesus addressed His disciples, He said that each one must take up his cross and follow Him (Matthew 16:24).

What does it mean to take up one's cross?

In Jesus's day, prisoners were forced to carry their own crosses to the location where they would be put to death. Thus, Christ's message was clear: In order to follow Him, His disciples must deny themselves and trust Him completely. Taking up one's cross means willingly embracing a life of surrender, sacrifice, and faithful obedience to Jesus, even when it's not easy.

For us today, this might look like forgiving someone who hurt us, serving others behind the scenes, or letting go of the control we have always held close. It's not about seeking pain or trouble but being willing to follow Jesus's words and example.

Do you seek to be a disciple of God's only begotten Son? Then pick up His cross today and every day that you live. In denying yourself, you will find fulfillment. In surrendering to Him, you will gain eternity.

Thinking Positive Thoughts

The idea of committed discipleship may be intimidating or overwhelming, but you can take at least one step today to become a better disciple for Christ. One prayer, one meditation, one act of kindness toward another person—each small effort moves you toward the path Jesus trod.

Remember This

To be a disciple of Christ means to follow in His footsteps—following His commandments, talking with Him often, telling others about Him, and sharing His never-ending love. Though your journey may be arduous at times, we have been promised that the path of Jesus leads to freedom, redemption, and joy.

If you've been waiting for the Lord, holding a promise from Him near to your heart, struggling at times because you think it's too late, use this time to cling to Him—to seek Him.

Kim Cash Tate

54

Defeating Procrastination

When you make a promise to God, don't delay in following through, for God takes no pleasure in fools. Keep all the promises you make to him.

Ecclesiastes 5:4 NLT

We can almost always find reasons to put off until tomorrow the things we should do today. But have you ever considered that there's never a "perfect" time to do anything?

We're all prone to procrastination, and for all sorts of reasons. Perhaps we put off a task because we doubt our ability to complete it well. Maybe you're overwhelmed, anxious, or simply dreading the job. Perfectionism can be a roadblock for many. But as we've said, perfect moments don't exist—and the longer you wait to do something, the greater the pressure builds.

Instead of hoping for the "right moment" to arrive, break the task into small, manageable steps. A complicated or long-term obligation may seem foreboding, but the first actionable item may seem much less intimidating. Grace for yourself, clear priorities, and inviting God into the process can help shift a halted pattern toward progress.

Together, you and the Father can accomplish great things . . . and with a mindset of resolve rather than delay, you can accomplish them more quickly—and easily—than you imagined.

Thinking Positive Thoughts

What have you been putting off that you know would be good for God's kingdom? If you are struggling to start something important, make an appointment for yourself and keep it. Then ask God to strengthen your resolve to begin. Once you *do* begin, you'll likely discover that the task you'd postponed was not nearly as daunting as your imagination made it out to be!

Remember This

To make the most of your talents—and to achieve your own personal goals—imagine procrastination as an obstacle in your way. Envision the end result of the work you've been delaying and use that satisfying vision as a motivator for your forward progress.

It is time to build new habits for a new context.
What would goodness look like in your life?
In your family? In your community? In our nation?
Dare to dream it. Then build it.

LISA HARPER

55

Praying for God's Abundance

I have come that they may have life, and that they may have it more abundantly.

John 10:10 NKJV

The familiar words of John 10:10 remind us that Christ came to this earth so we might experience His abundance, His love, and the gift of eternal life. But Christ does not force this gift upon us; we must accept what He offers.

Every woman knows what it feels like to be hanging on by a thread. We've experienced exhausting days and sleepless nights, when rejuvenating rest seemed like a distant promise. Perhaps you are feeling that way right now—depleted, hopeless, and anxious about tomorrow. In such seasons, you fantasize about having *enough*. Forget about having more than you need!

To believe in God's abundance means trusting that He is not limited by our circumstances, resources, or fears—and that He delights in caring generously for His children. Yes, His love is material in that it meets our physical needs, but it is also spiritually, emotionally, and eternally satisfying.

Today claim the only kind of abundance that really matters. Take the deep breaths you desperately need and ask your heavenly Father for guidance, rest, and protection. Will you claim His spiritual riches and experience His peace? You can and you should. God's abundance is available to all. Accept it and be blessed.

Thinking Positive Thoughts

Believing in God's abundance frees us from fear, comparison, and inadequate thinking. It helps us live with open hands—receiving with gratitude and giving without fear—because we know our Father's resources are never exhausted, and He will never let us go without.

Remember This

Abundant living may or may not include material wealth, but abundance always includes the spiritual riches you receive when you follow in the footsteps of Jesus. Today thank Him for the gifts you've already received—then live and give confidently, knowing He is far from done blessing you.

Knowing that your future is absolutely assured can free you to live abundantly today.

SARAH YOUNG

56

Trusting God's Wisdom

Sensible people keep their eyes glued on wisdom, but a fool's eyes wander to the ends of the earth.

PROVERBS 17:24 NLT

Who is the wisest person you know—and why does the word *wise* describe them? Wisdom is different from information or book smarts, and wisdom is not the same as natural-born intelligence. Wisdom, rather, is born of experience, gained through a lifetime of failures and resilience—which is why we often associate wisdom with elders who have "been around the block a few times."

Yet even the wisest among us cannot compare their knowledge to the omniscient and holy wisdom of God. God's wisdom is profoundly different from human wisdom because it is pure, eternal, and perfectly aligned with truth and love. While human wisdom is derived from experience, God's wisdom flows from His all-knowing nature. He sees the full picture, from beginning to end, so He knows what is truly best for us.

Though we ought to honor the wisdom of our elders—especially those who have devoted their lives to God—we must keep in mind that only God's mind is perfect. His will is eternal and unchanging, while human beings are fallible by nature. Let us put our faith instead in the One who never errs, who never causes confusion. Talk with Him; listen to Him; trust Him. He is your steadfast Protector, now and forever.

Thinking Positive Thoughts

Keep in mind that the world's wisdom often looks like "foolishness to God" (1 Corinthians 3:19). Though the people around you may wonder about your priorities, take heart in knowing that you are part of God's incredible upside-down kingdom.

Remember This

If we need wisdom right away, we need to look toward the example of Jesus. Scripture tells the story of perfection embodied on earth—of a man whose actions and heart demonstrate for us how to live in humility, righteousness, and love.

What we need is the actual wisdom of God.
We need a supernatural wisdom that
transcends what we know in the natural.

CHRISTINE CAINE

57

Being Kind, Compassionate, and Generous

May the Lord make your love for one another and for all people grow and overflow, just as our love for you overflows.

1 THESSALONIANS 3:12 NLT

Christ has been—and will always be—the ultimate friend to His flock. He spent His time on earth serving the outcast and the sick, and He showed His unconditional love for humankind by willingly sacrificing His life so we might have eternal life (Romans 5:8). As Christ's followers, we are not only challenged to share His love in the form of the gospel; we have also been instructed to love one another with kind words on our lips and praise in our hearts (John 13:34–35).

Jesus showed love throughout His life in ways that were radical, surprising, and sacrificial. He made friendship with people who had been judged harshly by their communities, and He healed people who had been afflicted for many years. He fed the hungry, and He cast out demons—all in the name of glorifying God and serving the people around Him.

Because Jesus is our example for living, it is good for us to be kind and compassionate toward others. Even more, it is right for our hearts to overflow with generosity because we've received such generous gifts of grace.

When we share the love of Christ, we share a priceless gift with the world. As devoted servants, it is our honor and privilege to do so.

Thinking Positive Thoughts

Kind thoughts are healthy thoughts, and kindness is contagious. When someone experiences an unexpected act of kindness, their defenses are softened, their spirits are lifted, and they often catch the desire to pass that goodness on to someone else.

Remember This

Kindness invites others into something better—specifically, into the way of Christ. Kindness tells people they matter. And when someone feels seen, loved, or encouraged, they're more likely to pass that light along.

By choosing love, we can foster connections
that uplift and encourage us.
Together, let us create a world where
kindness reigns, and love is our guiding principle.

Corrie ten Boom

58

Experiencing God's Grace

God saved you by his grace when you believed. And you can't take credit for this; it is a gift from God. Salvation is not a reward for the good things we have done, so none of us can boast about it.

Ephesians 2:8–9 NLT

God's grace is not earned. Thank goodness! To earn God's love and His gift of eternal life would be far beyond the abilities of even the most righteous person. Thankfully, grace is not an earthly reward for righteous behavior; it is a blessed spiritual gift which can be accepted by those who confess the name of Christ. When we accept Christ into our hearts, we are saved by His incredible grace.

The familiar words of Ephesians 2:8 make God's promise perfectly clear: By grace we have been saved, through faith.

Grace is at the very heart of the Christian life. Though a powerful theological concept, grace in practical terms is the foundation of our relationship with God, the fuel for our growth, and the motivator for living out our faith every day. Perhaps what's most powerful about grace is that it's not a one-off sort of gift; it renews us over and over, continually cleansing us and preparing us for an eternal life with our Father.

As we receive grace, we're called to extend it—to forgive, to show kindness, and to love our neighbors as ourselves (Matthew 22:39). A life touched by grace becomes a life that gives it away—and we return our Father's abundant gift by accepting His grace and by sharing His message and His love.

Thinking Positive Thoughts

Because God's grace is freely given, we no longer have to spend our effort trying to earn the unearnable. To accept the gift means acknowledging that no religious performance would save us. What saves us is Jesus crucified. Because of His great sacrifice, we live in freedom.

Remember This

Grace means we are loved, accepted, and forgiven not because we deserve it but because God is rich in mercy. Thanks to Jesus, we are free—empowered to live with boldness and joy!

What an honor it is to know, through God's grace, that you and I have been offered a position on his team—to serve the people He made and loved, and to share with them the love He promises.

Tasha Layton

59

Putting Bitterness Behind You

Hatred stirs up quarrels, but love makes up for all offenses.
Proverbs 10:12 NLT

Being frail, fallible, imperfect beings, most of us are quick to anger, quick to blame, slow to forgive, and even slower to forget. Yet we know Scripture tells us to forgive others, just as we, too, have been graciously forgiven.

Bitterness happens when we let our anger or disappointment fester. As we refuse or fail to address it, or as we shove it into the dark corners of our minds, the negative emotion grows. The result is a feeling that eats away at our hearts like a slow-acting poison or rot. The object of our bitterness never suffers though; only those of us who hold these grudges feel the ill effects of our choices. In a way, to cling to bitterness is to punish oneself. The damage is only felt by the one who cannot move on.

If there exists even one person—including yourself—against whom you still harbor bitter feelings, consider how much better you will feel without a grudge to feed and nurture. Bitterness has never been part of God's plan for you, but He won't force you to forgive others and forge a brand-new path. It's a job that only you can finish—and the sooner you finish it, the better.

Thinking Positive Thoughts

You can never fully enjoy the present if you're bitter about the past. So instead of dwelling on something you can't change, endeavor to make peace with it and carry on. Take what lessons you can from your experience. Then set your course on a fresh, new path.

Remember This

The cure for bitterness is a deep surrender to God's healing grace. First, honestly acknowledge the source of your bitterness. Next, ask for God's forgiveness. Finally, trust that His future plan for you is far better than anything negative you have already experienced.

Confidence in God's plan helps us to draw the conclusion that if we did not receive something it is because we did not need it.

Sarah Jakes Roberts

60

Rejoicing in the Lord

This is the day the Lord has made.
We will rejoice and be glad in it.
Psalm 118:24 NLT

We are blessed beyond measure. Even as we endure tough seasons of life, a woman of God would not be hard-pressed to look around and name her blessings—her friends, family, church community, the roof over her head, and many more earthly relationships and treasures. Additionally, each of us has received the gift of the Holy Spirit, and we will all inherit eternal life according to His promise. Even if we have lost everything, nothing can separate us from the love of Christ (Romans 8:31–39).

To cultivate a spirit or habit of gratitude, look no further than the book of Psalms. The Psalms are timeless because they speak to the deepest parts of the human soul—joy, sorrow, pain, hope, doubt, and worship—and point us back to God in every emotion and situation. These honest prayers—many of which were written by King David and all of which were inspired by the Holy Spirit—help us connect with God personally and powerfully. And many of the psalms model for us how to praise God through every circumstance.

Psalm 100 reminds us to "Shout for joy to the Lord, all the earth. Worship the Lord with gladness; come before him with joyful songs" (vv. 1–2 NIV). Psalm 118 reminds us that each day is a gift from the Creator. Do you have a favorite chapter or verse from the Psalms? If so, consider memorizing it or meditating upon it regularly. The power within these ancient words is as present with us as it was many thousands of years ago.

Thinking Positive Thoughts

Remember that every day, including this one, should be a cause for celebration. Which of the psalms you've read best demonstrates this spirit of divine gladness and exuberant cheer?

Remember This

When you celebrate God's gifts—when you place His promises firmly in your mind and your heart—you'll find yourself celebrating life. Through praise, you continually declare God's goodness, faithfulness, justice, mercy, and power.

Rejoicing in the Lord implies that you
have an intimate relationship with Him.
You can't rejoice in someone you don't know.

CHRISTINE CAINE

61

Following in Christ's Footsteps

Anyone who wants to serve me must follow me,
because my servants must be where I am.
And the Father will honor anyone who serves me.
John 12:26 NLT

Many people these days track their steps with a wristband or watch. "Just one more lap around the block!" walkers will say. "I'm trying to get my steps in!"

No matter whether you walk ten or ten thousand steps a day, Jesus walks with you. Are you walking with Him?

Jesus walked a lot during His time on earth, but perhaps one of His most distinctive walks was His journey across the Sea of Galilee to the boat carrying His disciples. As He approached them amid a storm at sea, the disciples assumed He was a ghost. But Jesus revealed Himself to them and even invited Peter to join Him on the waves (Matthew 14:22–33).

Walking on water was only one of many ways that Jesus revealed His divine nature to those who followed Him. But for us today, walking with Jesus can be a similarly adventurous journey. When we follow Him, we acknowledge His authority as our Savior and the Son of God. We take steps in faith we might not otherwise have taken, trusting that He will protect us and guide us. Ultimately, when we walk with Him, we agree to take up His cross and follow Him where He leads (Luke 9:23). When we do, we quickly discover that Christ's love has the power to change everything—including you and me.

Thinking Positive Thoughts

Ponder your relationship with Jesus: what it is and what it should be. Are you experiencing the peace and joyful abundance that is yours when you follow Him? Remember that Jesus came to His disciples amid the storm, just as He comes to you amid your storms. His presence doesn't always still the storm, but it brings peace in the midst of it.

Remember This

God blesses thoughtful believers who choose to follow Christ. Jesus is ready to lead you, but it's up to you to follow.

Discipleship is surrender . . . The salvation part is free, thank God. But discipleship costs.

Priscilla Shirer

62

Tuning Out the Noise

Serve only the Lord *your God and fear him alone.*
Obey his commands, listen to his voice, and cling to him.

Deuteronomy 13:4 NLT

In our world, simplicity is in short supply. Think for a moment about the complexity of your everyday life and compare it to the lives of your ancestors. We are the beneficiaries of many technological innovations, but those innovations tend to make a lot of (figurative) noise and don't always make life easier. Our attention these days is a commodity—a commodity everyone is trying to buy. Advertisements, news channels, and social networking sites are but a few of the voices begging for our attention. As a result, we are prone to all sorts of distractions and more worries than ever before. It's possible you may have learned from a headline today about something new to worry about that you'd never even thought about before!

There's nothing wrong with being informed, but we have to be the ones who take charge of our time and attention. You may already feel overwhelmed by an ever-increasing tidal wave of information that threatens your happiness and your sanity. But at the end of the day, your heavenly Father is the one who holds the world in His hands. He is in charge of many things over which we are ultimately powerless. He also understands the joy of living simply, and He promises peace to those whose souls need rest. So do yourself a favor: Take stock of who gets your attention and make sure God gets the most. You won't regret shutting out some of the noise and letting God's calm, caring voice soothe your soul.

Thinking Positive Thoughts

The ways to quiet the noise of the world can be pretty simple: turning off your phone and television, sitting somewhere quiet and comfortable, meditating over God's Word, and turning your thoughts to Him in prayer. Each of these habits invites peace into your spirit and makes it easier for you to hear God's voice.

Remember This

The simpler your life, the more you can focus on the things that really matter. Shutting out the world's noise and listening to God takes effort, but in a world filled with distractions, constant input, and pressures to stay busy, learning to quiet your heart and mind helps you better hear God's gentle voice.

The world may be loud and demanding, but the God you serve is ever-present, ever-faithful, and ever-worthy of your undivided attention." -

Christy Nockels

63

Making the Most of Whatever Comes

We can make our plans, but the LORD determines our steps.
PROVERBS 16:9 NLT

To be able to adapt and appear to be in control is important for the modern woman. We have a lot to manage—our homes, jobs, families, communities, and so much more. Our days may be scheduled to the hilt, and we may be the most organized women in the world—but sometimes life has a way of unfolding in a way that does *not* cooperate with the calendar. Sometimes these surprises are serendipitous, but sometimes they are not—and there is little we can do to change things.

When events transpire that are beyond our control, we are faced with a choice: to learn the art of acceptance or to make ourselves miserable as we struggle to change the unchangeable. For some of us, the problem lies in knowing what can (or should) be changed. The well-known Serenity Prayer puts this perfectly: "God grant me the serenity to accept things I cannot change, courage to change things I can, and wisdom to know the difference."

Despite our inclination to hold the reins, we must entrust the things we cannot change to God. If we don't, we'll find ourselves expending a lot of energy on what will be a fruitless endeavor. If you are in a place today where life is throwing you curveballs, prayerfully ask God for acceptance so you can faithfully tackle the rest of the important work He has placed before you. Then take a deep breath, thank Him for His help, and trust Him to accomplish what only He can.

Thinking Positive Thoughts

As God's daughters, we believe God is in control of the world, even when life feels uncertain or disappointing. Making the most of each moment means trusting that God can use *all things*—both joyful and painful—for His glory and our good (Romans 8:28). He can even use these moments of surrender to teach us new and life-changing lessons.

Remember This

When you encounter situations you cannot change, try to remember that God is faithful and has a marvelous plan for your life. Part of becoming a mature Christian is learning to accept the things you cannot change and learning to trust God in every situation.

When the pain, memories, and what-ifs overwhelm you, surrender them to God . . . Give God what you yourself cannot bear.

Anne Wilson

64

Taking Advantage of Each New Day

The one sitting on the throne said,
"Look, I am making everything new!"
Revelation 21:5 NLT

When you are faced with uncertainties, threats, or something new, what is your typical response? Do you size up the situation before making a rational move? Or do you tend to fight, flee, or freeze at the notion of trying something you've never tried?

Each new day offers countless new things—opportunities to serve God, to seek His will, and to follow His teachings. How will we, as daughters of the Highest, choose to respond to those opportunities?

Sometimes we wander aimlessly in a wilderness of our own making—but God has better plans for us. Consequently, whenever we ask Him to renew our strength and guide our steps, He is always there for us.

Each day there is a new beginning for you and me. Consider each morning a fresh start, a renewed opportunity to serve your Creator with willing hands and a loving heart. If you feel you are wandering, ask the Lord to renew your sense of purpose. Ask Him for courage, guidance, and for the wisdom to trust your hopes rather than your fears. When you ask, you will receive because He always keeps His promises. Always.

Thinking Positive Thoughts

Though we tend to prefer our predictable and comfortable situations, consider that any new opportunity that presents itself might be a God-given one. If an opportunity piques your interest or lights up your spirit, resist the temptation to ignore it. Ask God to show you whether this chance is one He has specifically chosen for you.

Remember This

If you're contemplating a major change, slow down, and pray for God's guidance. Look beyond the present moment with confidence, knowing that God has equipped you for any task He places before you.

Sometimes we have to wait on God. Other times we have to jump at opportunities even though they don't look the way we thought they should look.

TASHA LAYTON

65

Praying When You Feel Anxious

Worry weighs a person down;
an encouraging word cheers a person up.
PROVERBS 12:25 NLT

When calamity strikes anywhere in the world, we are often confronted with real-time images that breed worry, anxiety, or fear. And as we stare transfixed at our screens, we may fall prey to despair. Sometimes the grief in front of us is too much to take in, leaving us feeling numb or overwhelmed. Over time, these feelings build up, and it only makes sense that our souls are wounded by the thought of so much suffering.

Our Father in heaven knows the burdens we bear on behalf of ourselves and others, and He has promised us lives of abundance despite the fallen ways of the world. In fact, His Word instructs us not to "worry about anything" (Philippians 4:6 NLT)—a command that seems almost impossible to keep. So why did God provide us this directive? So we would bring our fears to Him and leave them in His capable hands.

If you find yourself becoming anxious or distraught, though you long for a spirit of peace, do your best to turn your concerns over to your heavenly Father. Though the world may seem to be pulling apart at the seams, we worship the God who created the universe and continues to hold it all together. He will comfort you if you ask Him—so ask Him, trust Him, and then experience the amazement as your anxieties begin to melt away.

Thinking Positive Thoughts

Most of us are prone to worrying and catastrophizing. But how productive are our worries? In His Sermon on the Mount, Jesus asked the people, "Can all your worries add a single moment to your life?" (Matthew 6:27). We know the answer to that is no—so resolve to let God take care of a future that only He can see.

Remember This

Remembering God's faithfulness in the past can give you peace for today and hope for tomorrow. If you are feeling anxious today, try dwelling on a moment when God took care of you. Then lay your latest worries at His feet.

Anxiety is a thin stream of fear trickling through the mind. If encouraged, it cuts a channel into which all other thoughts are drained.

PRISCILLA SHIRER

66

Finding Contentment in All the Right Places

Yes, I am the gate. Those who come in through me will be saved. They will come and go freely and will find good pastures.

John 10:9 NLT

Where can we find contentment? Is it a result of wealth or power or beauty or fame? Hardly. Genuine contentment springs from a peaceful spirit, a clear conscience, and a loving heart. It comes from valuing the things of God and finding purpose in our daily walk with Him.

The world around us seems preoccupied with the search for happiness and satisfaction. We are promised that if we buy this product, it will solve our problems. If we follow this step-by-step plan, we will be healthier and happier in no time. These messages make big claims that are usually expensive and almost always disappointing. We will never be able to purchase peace; rather, peace is the inevitable result of spending time the Father.

To be content means learning to rest in God's presence, trust in His provision, and believe He is enough for us (and that we are enough for Him). It's not found in getting everything we want but in knowing who we belong to and where our true security lies. The things of earth will all pass away, but we worship an unchanging God who promises us an eternal future. Why would we trust in things that disappear when God's promises are forever?

Thinking Positive Thoughts

Have you ever heard the expression "Comparison is the thief of joy"? It's a common expression because it's true! Nothing steals your contentment like comparing yourself to someone else. But remember, God didn't create you to live someone else's story. When you embrace your unique journey with God, you find peace and satisfaction in *your* path—the one He designed for you.

Remember This

The search for contentment is an internal quest, an exploration of the heart, mind, and soul—and thankfulness especially shifts your focus from what's lacking to what you've already been given. Regularly naming your blessings, big and small, reminds your heart that you're cared for and not forgotten.

The key to contentment is to consider.
Consider who you are and be satisfied with that.
'Consider what you have and be satisfied with that.
Consider what God's doing and be satisfied with that.

LUCI SWINDOLL

67

Choosing Cheerfulness

A cheerful heart has a continual feast.

Proverbs 15:15 HCSB

Cheerfulness is not always our default state. As the demands of the world increase and our energy sags, we feel less like "cheering up" and more like "tearing up."

As a Christian, cheerfulness is not about ignoring hardship or faking a smile; it's about rooting your joy and salvation in Christ rather than your circumstances. As a spiritual posture, cheerfulness flows from trust, gratitude, and hope in an eternal future. When we choose to reflect the light of Christ, even when life feels dark or uncertain, the natural outpouring of that choice is joy.

Yes, we are all sad at times. Even Christians are prone to bouts of grumpiness. But when we focus on who God is—His faithfulness, kindness, and unwavering goodness—our hearts find plenty of reasons to rejoice.

How can we receive from Christ the joy that is rightfully ours? By giving Him what is rightfully His: our hearts and our souls. Choose a cheerful heart by looking for God's hand in everything that's good and bad. That way, even amid your most challenging seasons, you will find the kind of resilient joy that flows freely from believing in His promises.

Thinking Positive Thoughts

If you've ever been around a joyful person, you know that cheerfulness and joy is contagious. So if you need a little cheering up, go find someone to encourage. When you brighten somebody else's day, it lightens your heart and reflects joy back to you.

Remember This

Good cheer (joy) is one of the fruits of the Spirit (Galatians 5:22). The more time you spend in prayer, Scripture, and quiet meditation, the more joy naturally rises in your soul.

The secret to joy, no matter what,
is to always find the good in everything.

ANN VOSKAMP

68

Praying Specifically for the Things You Need

Always be joyful. Never stop praying.
Be thankful in all circumstances, for this is
God's will for you who belong to Christ Jesus.

1 Thessalonians 5:16–18 NLT

As the old saying goes, if it's big enough to worry about, it's big enough to pray about. Yet sometimes, we don't pray about the specific details of our lives. Instead, we may offer general prayers that are decidedly heavy on platitudes and decidedly light on particulars.

The next time you pray, try this: Be very specific about the things you ask God to do. Of course, God already knows precisely what you need—He knows infinitely more about your life than you do—but you need the experience of talking to your Creator in honest, straightforward language.

So today, don't be vague with God. Tell Him exactly what you need. He doesn't need to hear the details, but you do.

Thinking Positive Thoughts

There's no corner of your life that's too unimportant to pray about, so pray about everything. When you do, God will guide your path and direct your thoughts in the proper direction.

Remember This

God does not answer all our prayers in the affirmative, nor should He. When we are disappointed by the realities of life-here-on-earth, we should remember that our prayers are always answered by a sovereign, all-knowing God and that we must trust Him, whether He answers, "Yes," "No," or "Not yet."

When we pray specifically, we're showing God that we've thought carefully about what we're asking and that we truly believe He can provide it.

Margaret Feinberg

69

Facing Problems with God's Help

The righteous person faces many troubles, but the LORD comes to the rescue them from each time.

PSALM 34:19 NLT

Spoiler alert: The upcoming day will not be problem free! You might lock your keys in the minivan when you're running late to a meeting. Your kid could get in trouble at school, meaning you have the "privilege" of a one-on-one meeting with his teacher *and* the principal. Whether filled with big or small annoyances, this day in your life can be viewed as an exercise in problem-solving or a test in mental and emotional fortitude. The question is not *whether* you will encounter problems but rather *how* you will choose to address them.

When it comes to solving the problems of everyday living, we often know precisely what needs to be done. But what about the perplexing circumstances—the problems that seem unsolvable? The problems that overwhelm us?

The words of Psalm 34 remind us that the Lord solves problems for believers who trust Him. Yes, He has equipped us with skills and abilities to live powerfully and capably from day to day—but the situations that demand His divine intervention provide precious opportunities to draw nearer to Him.

Do what you can and let God do the rest. He is willing and more than able!

Thinking Positive Thoughts

Today think about the wisdom of tackling certain problems

sooner rather than later. Which ones are demanding your attention today, and which ones demand God's help? Fretting about problems is not the same as addressing them—so ask God for assistance as you tackle the problems you face.

Remember This

With God on your side, no problem is unsolvable, no obstacle too big to overcome. Use the many skills and strengths He has given you to make the most of your situation. Then relax in the knowledge that God can handle the rest.

No problem is too big for God to handle.
With Him by your side, you can overcome
any obstacle that comes your way.

Francesca Battistelli

Putting Faith Above Feelings

Now the just shall live by faith.

Hebrews 10:38 NKJV

Do you forget sometimes that you are in charge of your emotions? At times, we let our emotions get the best of us. Or even worse, we let other people or external factors determine the quality of our thoughts and the direction of our days.

Emotions are healthy and useful, and they are essential to the human experience. After all, what would life be like without happiness, sadness, and the more complicated feelings? But our emotions are highly variable, decidedly unpredictable, and often unreliable. Our emotions change like the weather, and not always for obvious reasons. Though feelings are not to be ignored, we must learn to live by a more reliable compass: the unchanging truth of God's promises.

Sometime during this day, you will probably be tempted to react to someone who crosses your path. Examine your natural reaction and then turn it over to God. Your emotions about that person will inevitably change, but God will not. As we grow in Him, may He give us the everyday ability to use our feelings for good—reacting and responding in ways to others that are God-glorifying and useful for His kingdom.

Thinking Positive Thoughts

Make a concerted effort to get to know the patterns of your emotions. For example, acknowledge if you should or shouldn't make big decisions when you're tired, stressed, or hungry. Or if you find yourself wanting to lash out at someone, try taking calming breaths and waiting awhile to compose yourself before speaking. Though we are adults here, sometimes we need "time-outs" too. Don't try to ignore or defeat your emotions but learn how to use them in ways that honor God.

Remember This

We can usually trust our instincts, but we can *always* trust God. May we learn to live to the fullest by entrusting our emotions and reactions to the One who never changes.

Feelings can be fickle, but your Heavenly Father's love for you is steadfast and true. Place your trust in Him.

Rebecca St. James

Pleasing God, Not the World

Obviously, I'm not trying to win the approval of people, but of God. If pleasing people were my goal, I would not be Christ's servant.

Galatians 1:10 NLT

Christian women seem to have perfected the art of pleasing people. With good intentions, women work hard to serve others and pick up the slack whenever needed. But what happens when our good intentions evolve, and we begin avoiding conflict or trying to earn approval at any cost?

If you are like most women, you've likely found yourself agreeing to something in order to avoid disappointing someone else. But when we are *too* agreeable, we may find ourselves spending too much time, energy, or money on things that are detracting from our unique purposes in God. To avoid hard conversations, are we compromising our callings? We should check our motivations to see if we've crossed the line from serving others to pleasing people.

The Bible calls us to serve others, care for them, and show kindness—but that doesn't mean saying yes to everything or avoiding healthy boundaries. Nor does it mean compromising our values or beliefs to make others happy. While service is Christian virtue, God also calls women to live boldly, speak truth, and follow Him first. In all you do, make sure your motive is to please God above all.

Thinking Positive Thoughts

If you find yourself feeling guilty about making and keeping a boundary, remember that Jesus set a good example for us. Though a multitude of people sought Him for healing, He prioritized His prayer time alone (Luke 5:15–16). We, too, can say no sometimes. After all, we're only human and it is healthy to balance your yes and nos.

Remember This

Trying to keep everyone happy can be downright stressful. So do yourself a favor: Try to worry less about everyone else's feelings while you prioritize spiritual realities. God called you to love people—not guarantee their contentment!

We must not confuse the command to love with the disease to please.

Lysa TerKeurst

72

Recognizing the Value of Obedience

"Not everyone who calls out to me, 'Lord! Lord!' will enter the Kingdom of Heaven. Only those who actually do the will of my Father in heaven will enter."

MATTHEW 7:21 NLT

God's laws are eternal and unchanging. How do we know this? Because He has graciously given us a guidebook for righteous living in the form of His holy Word. If we trust the words of the Bible, we know He loves us, He knows what's best for us, and He has purpose for our lives that is greater than anything we could dream up on our own. Obedience is the act of taking those beliefs and putting them into practice.

Each day we make countless decisions that can bring us closer to God. Do you seek God's peace and His blessings by following His commands? When faced with a difficult choice or a powerful temptation, do you seek God's counsel through prayer and the Word? The commands and guidance found in the Bible are not arbitrary rules from God but rather divine protections and blessings. If we trust and follow the Word, we will experience wholeness rather than regret or harm.

Jesus said, "If you love me, obey my commandments" (John 14:15 NLT). What better way to demonstrate our love for Jesus, our trust in His promises, and our gratitude for His perfect sacrifice than to walk obediently in His footsteps?

Thinking Positive Thoughts

Many of God's commands involve how we treat others—meaning our faithful obedience trickles down to others. When we are kind, generous, selfless, and peaceful, those postures encourage others, show God's character to the world, and open doors for His love to spread.

Remember This

Our selfish or harmful actions have consequences, but God blesses us when we obey His Word.

When we walk in obedience, we stay in step with Him and experience greater clarity, peace, and joy from day to day.

There is nothing—no activity, no good deeds, no ministry work, no platform, no measure of influence—that can take the place of abiding. Of having a rich prayer life. Of listening and being sensitive to the leading of the Spirit. Of leaning into the Scriptures to understand the heartbeat of your Lord. Of being obedient to His directives.

Priscilla Shirer

73

Finding a Church Community

God has put all things under the authority of Christ and has made him head over all things for the benefit of the church. And the church is his body; it is made full and complete by Christ, who fills all things everywhere with himself.

Ephesians 1:22–23 NLT

If you have been considering joining a church, let this reading be a sign to you that *today* is the day! Endeavor this week to find a church family. Jesus established the church, the body of Christ, for many reasons—one being so we could worship Him together and multiply our collective joy.

Church is a wonderful place to grow spiritually, form friendships, find and build social safety nets, learn more about Scripture, and discover our unique callings. When part of a church family, we are exposed to opportunities to serve others that might never be possible outside a community. We can become accountable to others while they become accountable to us. These relationships are meant to strengthen everyone involved while also mimicking the kind of spiritual community we might all get to experience together in heaven.

Take the next step: Find a church you're comfortable with and get involved. And if you're already a faithful member of a church, look for ways to become more involved and deepen your relationships. Time spent worshiping God with others will bring joy to your heart and satisfaction to your spirit. We all need encouragement from time to time—and a beloved church home is a wonderful place to find it.

Thinking Positive Thoughts

Adding something to the to-do list can automatically turn that thing into *work.* So as you endeavor to find a new church family (or level up your current church involvement), strive to make church attendance a celebration not an obligation. The attitude you bring to the worship service may be just as important as the message you hear.

Remember This

Church is a great place to collect your thoughts, focus on your priorities, and recharge your spiritual batteries. At church, you'll find people to pray with, stand with, serve with, grow with, and walk through life with. As a member of the church family, you'll be encouraged, challenged, and supported in ways you can't experience on your own.

Every time a new person comes to God, every time someone's gifts find expression in the fellowship of believers, every time a family in need is surrounded by the caring church, the truth is affirmed anew: the Church triumphant is alive and well!

Gloria Gaither

74

Accountability with Grace

Do all that you can to live in peace with everyone.
ROMANS 12:18 NLT

We will all find ourselves in the wrong sometimes. Maybe we slip up and let our anger or selfishness take over, and at times, we wrong others by mistake. As broken people in a broken world, we will inevitably hurt one another; the question is how we will respond to the role we have personally played in the brokenness.

As Christians, we have been tasked with taking a higher road. We don't skirt our responsibilities by ignoring our errors; rather, we are called to ask for forgiveness and make peace with our neighbors. Taking accountability for wrongs is a powerful step toward healing, growth, and restoring relationships. It's also an act of humility and obedience—acknowledging our personal need for God's grace as we seek to live in truth and love.

If you have wronged someone, don't become paralyzed by guilt. Rather, do your best to make things right by confessing to God and then apologizing to the hurt party. Avoid blame-shifting or minimizing the situation; name what you did clearly and truthfully. Then rest in the thought that Christ's forgiveness covers everything. Thanks to His precious gift, not one of us is without hope of grace and redemption.

Thinking Positive Thoughts

A good apology articulates regret, responsibility, and a desire to make it right. An authentic apology listens quietly to grievances and doesn't attempt to defend itself. A true apology provides ample space for the other person to express how they were affected. Listening with humility shows respect and empathy, proving to the other person that the apology is real.

Remember This

Taking accountability may be challenging, but it's also freeing. It invites grace into your life and into your relationships, and it shows the world that your faith is real in word *and* in action.

When we, weak and without hope in our own strength, choose to come under the shelter of God's forgiveness through the blood of Christ, we are made strong in the Lord.

Ruth Chou Simons

75

Moving Mountains with God's Help

"I tell you the truth, you can say to this mountain, 'May you be lifted up and thrown into the sea,' and it will happen. But you must really believe it will happen and have no doubt in your heart."

MARK 11:23 NLT

When a chronically ill woman sought healing by simply touching the hem of Christ's garment, He turned to her and said, "Daughter, be encouraged! Your faith has made you well" (Matthew 9:22 NLT). We learn from Scripture that this woman had "suffered for twelve years"—only to be miraculously healed in an instant (v. 20). Whether we are physically or spiritually in need, we, too, can be transformed when we place our faith completely and unwaveringly in Jesus Christ.

To be transformed by Christ means living with bold, faith-filled dependence on God—trusting Him to do what we cannot and allowing Him to reshape our hearts, desires, and lives from the inside out. When we step out in faith, we are promised miraculous results. Moving mountains begins with believing that God is powerful, present, and willing to work through us—even when the obstacles before us appear overwhelming. While our powers are finite, God's are not. With His help, great things can be accomplished.

If you are facing a test to your faith, be content to touch even the smallest fragment of the Master's garment. His presence and divine power will make you whole.

Thinking Positive Thoughts

When God transforms His children, He gives us courage where fear once lived, love where bitterness once dwelled, and peace where discontentment once reigned. And through that transformation, He moves mountains—both in you and through you.

Remember This

This day, like every other day, is cause for optimism and hope because all things are possible with God. When you place your faith in your heavenly Father, life becomes a grand adventure energized by His limitless power. When you trust Him completely, get ready for miraculous things to happen.

When you and I place our faith in Jesus Christ and invite Him to come live within us, the Holy Spirit comes upon us, and the power of God overshadows us, and the life of Jesus is born within us.

Anne Graham Lotz

76

Understanding the Power of Silence

Truly my soul silently waits for God;
From Him comes my salvation.
Psalm 62:1 NKJV

Take a moment to pause and observe the sights and sounds around you. Are they peaceful? Attention-seeking? Are they uplifting and engaging, or exhausting and irritating? Are they sights and sounds you'd rather tune out and ignore?

The world seems to grow louder day by day, assaulting our senses and invading our peace. Implied in this bright, noisy world is the expectation that we will make ourselves be seen and heard. We figuratively wave our arms and shout our opinions over the commotion. If we want to make it in this world, we learn, we must be *as loud* or *louder than* the noise.

God's nature reminds us that the loudest, shiniest, and biggest is not the worthiest of attention. In fact, sometimes the steadfast and quiet person is the deepest and most intentional. Quiet people often listen more than they speak—a habit that gives them insight, empathy, and wisdom in their relationships. Their calm presence provides safety and builds connection. And because they are not rushing to fill a quiet moment, they are better able to take in and understand the person who is speaking.

Let's not confuse noise with power. Rather, let's look for strength in the stillness. After all, God works powerfully without saying a word—so let's quiet our minds and our hearts, listen for His will, and do our best to become the kind of listener who makes others feel safe and secure.

Thinking Positive Thoughts

Quiet individuals often offer more measured, meaningful responses in conversation, because they tend to reflect before acting or speaking. Their words also carry weight, not because they say a lot, but because they speak with care and conviction. In a world where silence is in short supply, let's refrain from speaking just to speak. Silence is, indeed, golden.

Remember This

A quiet spirit is not the same as weakness. Rather, in a world that often rewards size and volume, the quiet person holds a different kind of power—one that leads by example without demanding attention. Their faithfulness and attentiveness speak louder than words ever could.

When we learn to embrace the power of silence,
we discover a deeper, more profound connection
with the God who speaks to us in the stillness.

CHRISTY NOCKELS

77

Saying No to Anger

And "don't sin by letting anger control you." Don't let the sun go down while you are still angry, for anger gives a foothold to the devil.

Ephesians 4:26–27 NLT

Anger can be an appropriate response when one is faced with injustice or great harm. Even Jesus, our perfect Savior, became angry when confronted with the moneychangers in the temple. On occasion, like Jesus, you will be confronted with evil, and when you are, a similarly vigorous response would be in order. But, most of the time, your frustrations will be of the more mundane variety.

The difference between run-of-the-mill anger and righteous anger has to do with the object and nature of the offense. Justified anger aligns with God's heart and justice, whereas everyday anger offends our personal preferences or pride. Righteous anger arises out of respect for what God has told us is right, good, and true; it's not about proving a point, settling a debate, or reacting to perceived slights. Righteous anger stands against sin, oppression, abuse, dishonesty, or anything that violates or harms God's people. Everyday anger is rarely productive and never leads to loving correction.

As long as you live here on earth, you will face countless opportunities to lose your cool over personal offenses—traffic jams, spilled cups of coffee, rude or inconsiderate comments, and even broken promises. When you are tempted to lose your temper over the minor inconveniences of life, try to remember that God would like us to live in peace with everyone (Romans 12:18). Turn away from anger, hatred, and bitterness. Then turn instead to God.

Thinking Positive Thoughts

Angry words are dangerous to your emotional and spiritual

health, not to mention your relationships. If you are tempted to respond in an angry manner, train yourself to take a break first. Take some deep breaths, take a walk, and wait awhile before returning that text or email. Even better, get a good night's sleep first. Odds are, your anger will have dissipated by morning.

Remember This

Anger, if allowed to fester, can rob you of contentment and peace. So if you find yourself imprisoned by a lingering, unresolvable anger, it's time to ask God (sincerely and often) to bind it and heal your heart.

"Anger can blind us to the blessings around us. Open your eyes to God's goodness instead."

JACI VELASQUEZ

78

Believing You Are Protected

Even when I walk through the darkest valley,
I will not be afraid, for you are close beside me.
Your rod and your staff protect and comfort me.
Psalm 23:4 NLT

Before David became the King of Israel, he spent a long, excruciating season fleeing for his life. For many months (and possibly years), King Saul—Israel's first king—pursued David and tried to kill him, perceiving him as a threat and a rival. As David lived the life of a fugitive, escaping from one remote place to the next, he wrote some of his most beloved psalms. Many of these psalms describe David's fear and desolation—but the thread tying these heartfelt songs together is David's faith in the God who protected him.

The next time you find yourself facing a fear-provoking situation, remember that the One who loved and protected David is also your personal Savior. Though David's journey was grueling, God used this season to shape him into the humble, courageous, and God-dependent man who would one day be king. Likewise, God can use any circumstance to your advantage, cultivating within you a period of growth and a sense of security you may have never experienced. Because God cares for you, you are protected. You will never face any obstacles alone.

Thinking Positive Thoughts

David learned to lead, to wait on God's timing, and to walk in obedience throughout his long exile. What lessons has God taught you amid an uncertain or fear-inducing situation? If you are facing your own dark valley, ask Him to guide you to a place where you can realize your full potential. Even if you fail, take heart in knowing the experience may free you from the fear of failure and fill you with new courage.

Remember This

David's season of being hunted by Saul is a powerful reminder that God often uses times of hardship to shape our hearts for future purpose—and that trusting Him in the wilderness leads to strength, wisdom, confidence, and deeper faith.

If you ask God for that courage,
He will give it to you. He will give you boldness.

LAUREN DAIGLE

79

Growing as a Believer

Rather, you must grow in the grace and knowledge of our Lord and Savior Jesus Christ. All glory to him, both now and forever! Amen.

2 Peter 3:18 NLT

When will we become "fully-grown" Christians? Hopefully never! That is, let's hope we keep growing each day until Jesus comes back or God calls us home.

To grow spiritually in Christ means to become more like Him in your thoughts, attitudes, and actions. It's the ongoing process of being shaped by the Holy Spirit, rooted in God's Word, and living in close relationship with Jesus. We will never become perfect—only Jesus was perfect—but we will be transformed with God's help into humbler, wiser, and more generous versions of ourselves. We can even become more patient, less prone to worry, and more courageous thanks to His divine, redemptive work. There is no limit to the growth possible through Christ.

Would you like a time-tested formula for spiritual growth? Here it is: Keep studying God's Word, leaning into His commandments, praying (and listening for answers), and living in the center of God's will. When you do, you'll never stay stuck for long.

Thinking Positive Thoughts

In the quiet moments when you open your heart to God, the One who made you keeps growing you. He gives you direction, perspective, wisdom, and courage. Only with His patient, loving help and care do we mature and evolve in our faith over time. If you have been following Jesus for a while, take a moment to look back at your journey and see how far He has brought you. If you are new in your faith, use this moment to envision what your life will look like as you mature in your walk. What do you hope God will teach you? Then ask Him for the guidance you need.

Remember This

Complete spiritual maturity is never achieved in a day, a year, or even a lifetime. Yet every new day presents opportunities for emotional and spiritual growth. We can, with God's help, be transformed—moment by moment and day by day—into the kind of woman who serves Him with gladness and brings glory to His holy name.

Don't be afraid of the pruning process.
God removes what's holding you back
so you can grow stronger.

KARI JOBE

80

Finding Strength When Times Are Tough

Be strong and courageous, and do the work.
Don't be afraid or discouraged,
for the LORD God, my God, is with you.
He will not fail you or forsake you.
1 CHRONICLES 28:20 NLT

When Jesus spoke to His disciples about the future, He did not promise them lives of ease or comfort. From what we know of His life and crucifixion, Jesus Himself endured sadness, temptation, and pain at many turns. "Here on earth you will have many trials and sorrows," He told the disciples. "But take heart, because I have overcome the world" (John 16:33 NLT). The first half of that verse is not nearly as important as the second. Yes, we will face trouble—but even more, we have aligned ourselves with the One who has overcome every darkness.

Even during our most despairing moments, we are not left without the promise of help. We can depend upon our friends, family, church community, and ultimately upon God. Every biblical warning about trials and tribulations is lined with gold in the form of hope for the future. Armed with the knowledge that God has saved us and has guaranteed our eternal futures, each of us can find the courage to face even the most challenging days with hopeful hearts and willing hands.

The next time you find your courage tested to the limit, remember that—thanks to the Father—you're stronger than you think. With God on your side, you have nothing to fear.

Thinking Positive Thoughts

If you trust God completely, you have every reason on earth—*and* in heaven—to live courageously. He has already overcome the world and every speck of the known (and unknown) universe. When you ponder the power of the Lord who loves you, how does that strengthen your resolve?

Remember This

Fear loses power when you remember God's character: He is faithful, powerful, loving, and present. When you trust Him and Him alone, He will never fail you because no threat or uncertainty can separate you from His hand.

"When you feel like you can't take another step, God will carry you through and restore your soul."

Christy Nockels

81

Trusting God's Timetable

God has made everything beautiful for its own time.
He has planted eternity in the human heart,
but even so, people cannot see the
whole scope of God's work from beginning to end.

Ecclesiastes 3:11 NLT

Do you have a calendar? The question is almost ridiculous because some of us have more than one! We have so many things to keep track of—appointments, meetings, deadlines, holidays—that to imagine living without a detailed, organized plan seems near impossible in the modern age. Without our carefully coordinated schedules, would anything ever get done?

Life can be easier when we have a plan. But what happens when God's plans don't look at all like ours?

God has created a world that unfolds according to His own timetable. His plan does not always happen in the way that we would like or at the time of our own choosing. When compared to *our* ideal schedule, His plans might even seem inconvenient. But our task as believing Christians is to wait patiently for God to reveal Himself. Trusting God's timing instead of our own means letting go of control, surrendering our sense of urgency, and believing God's plan is not only better but also beautifully timed for our growth, good, and His glory. In short, to accept and trust in God's timing takes a great step of faith.

God is wise, loving, and never late. But until His perfect plan is made known, we must walk in faith and never lose hope. Today's disappointments may be preparing us for His greatest triumphs. For today, try to remember that God still has divine appointments in store for you.

Thinking Positive Thoughts

Instead of worrying about your future and replaying an unchangeable past, entrust the whole span of your life to God. Since He sees the full picture of human existence, He knows exactly what you need *and* exactly when you need it. What belongs to you and is purposed *for* you will happen according to His perfect schedule.

Remember This

You don't know precisely what you need—or when you need it—but God does. We may try to rush ahead because we feel like "nothing is happening." But trust means serving, learning, waiting, and growing where you are, believing that God is working even when we can't see it.

What if the first thing we meditated on in the morning was God's trustworthiness and His powerful ability to lead us by His Spirit at every turn? What if that was our starting place?

Ellie Holcomb

82

Loving Jesus as Your Best Friend

Those who obey God's word truly show how completely they love him. That is how we know we are living in him. Those who say they live in God should live their lives as Jesus did.

1 John 2:5–6 NLT

Who's the best friend this world has ever had? Jesus, of course. And when you form a life-changing relationship with Him, He will be your best friend too.

In John 15:15, Jesus acknowledges His disciples as His confidants and friends. How does it feel to know that you can count the Son of God as your ally? Jesus not only has offered us His presence and perfect example, but also He has promised to share the gifts of selfless love and everlasting life. If you make mistakes, He stands by you. If you fall short of His commandments, He still accepts you. If you feel lonely or worried, He can touch your heart and lift your spirits. To be friends with Jesus means being rooted in love, trust, honesty, and a shared life. His offer is not a distant or formal connection but an invitation to walk with Him daily, knowing He chooses you and delights in being close to you.

Jesus wants you to enjoy a happy, healthy, abundant life. And with a friend like Jesus, that's exactly what you will have.

Thinking Positive Thoughts

Our earthly friendships are blessings, but Jesus is the perfect friend to all. Through the conversation of prayer, you can talk to

Jesus openly and without shame or judgment. He wants to hear from you—not just the "right" words, but the real ones—and when you trust Him with your hopes, fears, and failures, He always listens, comforts, and guides. He will never let us down.

Remember This

To be friends with Jesus is to live in the comfort of His love, the security of His presence, and the joy of knowing you are never alone. He is the most faithful, understanding, and loving friend you will ever have.

What we can count on,
what He does promise us, is His love.

Rebecca St. James

83

Making the Most of Suffering

God is our refuge and strength,
a very present help in trouble.
PSALM 46:1 NKJV

Because we live in a broken and fallen world, suffering and adversity are inevitable. We spend a lot of time and effort seeking comfort and predictable circumstances, but some trials can't be avoided no matter what we do. Women of each generation face unique challenges that previous generations could have scarcely imagined, but thankfully, though the world continues to change, God's love for us stays the same. He also remains ready to comfort us and strengthen us whenever we turn to Him in need.

Perhaps the only good news about our pain and suffering is that God refuses to waste it. In His love and wisdom, He uses our struggles to shape, strengthen, and bless us—often in ways we can't see in the moment but that unfold over time with deep purpose.

When we are in pain, we are more likely to depend on the Father. Our desperate need draws us toward Him, resulting in a closeness with Him we may have never experienced. God also tends to take our brokenness and transform it into strength. Where we once believed we were vulnerable, we are suddenly courageous with God's help. And our suffering has a way of clarifying what is eternal and what is temporary; it helps us focus on what really lasts: faith, hope, love, and our relationship with God.

Take your troubles, pain, and weaknesses to Him. He is trustworthy and will shelter you through the storm.

Thinking Positive Thoughts

If you have ever bonded with someone over a shared pain, you know your wounds can become sources of comfort and wisdom for someone else. How is God using your pain to bring healing to someone else? Has someone else's pain ever made you feel less alone and helped you in the healing process?

Remember This

When you experience adversity, be encouraged that God can use anything you endure for good.

Your suffering is not meaningless or invisible. In God's hands, your pain can become an instrument for transformation, compassion, and even beauty.

Grace is unmerited favor. Grace is here for you right now, in the middle of what is hard or not working.

SHEILA WALSH

84

Searching for Wisdom

Now if any of you lacks wisdom, he should ask God, who gives to all generously and without criticizing, and it will be given to him. But let him ask in faith without doubting. For the doubter is like the surging sea, driven and tossed by the wind.

James 1:5–6 HCSB

Where do you go for wisdom when you need it? Do you seek out elders, mentors, or time-tested friends? In this life, we can never get enough wisdom, so having many sources to consult is convenient and a privilege. But part of being a devoted Christian is knowing the ultimate source of wisdom: our God and His Word.

Wisdom is more than knowledge, facts, aphorisms, or clichés; it's the ability to see life from God's perspective and live accordingly. Though we search for some types of answers from others or the world around us, true wisdom begins with reverence for God (Proverbs 9:10). It comes when we quiet our thoughts, open His Word, study the Scriptures, and ask for clarity. We especially need divine counsel as we face big decisions, but we can also use everyday wisdom to honor and glorify Him with our lives.

Today, as you prepare yourself for the inevitable ups and downs of everyday life, remember that God's wisdom can be found in a book that's already on your bookshelf: His Book. Read and live accordingly. You can never glean enough wisdom from the Father.

Thinking Positive Thoughts

To acquire wisdom is the first step; the next step is to take wise actions. Good intentions are wonderful, but they are useless if never acted upon. Once you've sought God's guidance and gained insight through His Word, act on it with faith and courage. What is one step of faith you can take today that represents His wisdom moving forward in action?

Remember This

Wisdom is the application of truth in such a way that it results in skillful, effective, powerful living. When we actively respond to God's gifts of wisdom—whether that means extending forgiveness, speaking truth in love, or stepping into a new calling—we begin to reflect His heart more clearly in the world.

Wisdom is knowledge applied. Head knowledge is useless on the battlefield. Knowledge stamped on the heart makes one wise.

Beth Moore

85

Pursuing Joy

Make me hear joy and gladness.

Psalm 51:8 NKJV

The joy the world offers is fleeting and incomplete—here today, gone tomorrow, and maybe never returning. But God's joy is different. His joy has staying power. In fact, the joy of salvation in Christ is a gift that never stops giving to those who welcome Jesus into their hearts.

Amid the inevitable complications and predicaments woven into the fabric of everyday life, we sometimes forget to rejoice. We get wrapped up in our obligations and don't make time to appreciate our blessings. Or instead of celebrating life, we complain about its minor inconveniences. As Christians experiencing daily redemption, we have every reason to live joyfully and abundantly. To do otherwise is to belittle or even squander His many spiritual gifts.

Pursuing joy—especially as a Christian—is not about ignoring hardship, but rather about anchoring our hearts in the truth of who God is. Joy is among the fruit of the Spirit (Galatians 5:22), and when we pursue it, we are intentionally dwelling on our blessings instead of anything that might topple our posture of gratitude. Thanking God for His blessings shifts our focus from what's lacking to what's present—and the woman who contents herself through gratitude will find herself with unshakable joy.

This day and every day, Christ offers you His holy gifts. Accept His offerings and share them with others, just as He has shared them with you.

Thinking Positive Thoughts

Joy isn't always found in grand events. You can often find it in a kind word, a warm cup of coffee, or a quiet moment with God. Looking for the beauty in nature or other people cultivates joy. Taking a short walk, singing a song you love, and laughing at a joke are all small efforts you can make each day that remind you that life is, indeed, a divine gift.

Remember This

Remember that joy begins with a choice—the choice to establish a genuine relationship with God and His Son. Joy does not depend upon your circumstances but upon the blessings you have received, thanks to your relationship with God.

Thanks is what multiplies the joy and makes any life large.

Ann Voskamp

86

Finding Fulfillment in Heavenly Things

Then he said, "Beware! Guard against every kind of greed. Life is not measured by how much you own."

Luke 12:15 NLT

How should a believer think about material possessions? As flesh-and-blood people with physical needs, we need the basic necessities of life. But once we meet those needs for ourselves and for our families, the piling up of possessions can create more problems than it solves. Our real riches, of course, are not of this world. We are never truly rich until we are rich in spirit.

Jesus's life and the example of the early church demonstrate for us that earthly possessions should not be a source of identity or security. Instead, they are temporary tools to be used for serving others, glorifying God, and advancing His eternal kingdom.

Jesus Himself lived simply, traveling from place to place and carrying very little as He preached and healed the sick. The Bible tells us He had "no place even to lay his head" (Luke 9:58 NLT), and He spoke often of valuing heavenly treasures over earthly goods (Matthew 6:19–21). Likewise, the members of the early church were committed to sharing with each other, going so far as to sell what they had to cover each other's needs (Acts 2:44–45). Together these examples show us that possessions are meant to be held loosely, with open hands and generous hearts.

Philippians 4:8 reminds us of what we should value: "what is true, and honorable, and right, and pure, and lovely, and admirable" (NLT). When the heavenly things fill up our hearts and thoughts, the things of this earth will naturally—and rightly—lose their allure.

Thinking Positive Thoughts

Do you find yourself wrapped up in the concerns of the material world? If so, practice decentering those concerns by doing without from time to time. Rather than buying something new, try using what you already have. If you have more of something than you need, look for ways to donate it charitably rather than pocketing it for later. Generous, humble, and simple living brings about its own satisfying spiritual benefits.

Remember This

Material possessions have a way of dominating our thoughts. As a consequence, the things we own may seem very important to us—but they are not as important to God. He's concerned with your heart, not your status or wealth. And you can be sure: The things you own aren't nearly as important as the person you're becoming.

True fulfillment isn't found in having more,
but in needing less and loving God more.

JACI VELASQUEZ

87

Treating Each Day as a Gift

We must quickly carry out the tasks assigned us by the one who sent us. The night is coming, and then no one can work.

John 9:4 NLT

Not all days are created equal. Some seem easy-breezy, while others feel like uphill battles from dawn 'til dusk. While it might seem obvious which of these days most feels like a gift from God, be honest for a moment: When things are going especially well, do you pause to dwell on the blessed direction of that day? Or do you look back on the simpler days during the difficult times and think, *If only I'd known how good I had it back then?*

Whatever the nature of the day (bad or good), we are always living in the present—a moment full of its own gifts and possibilities, whether we acknowledge them or not. When the days are easy, we tend to take the ease for granted, and when the days are tough, we tend to wish that time away. In either case, we are forfeiting an opportunity: the chance to look around us and count our blessings, to appreciate the unique potential God has embedded in each day of our lives.

How will you invest this day? Will you treat your time as a commodity too precious to be squandered, or will you spin your wheels wishing your circumstances were different? Will you carve out time during the day to serve God and His children, or will you waste time by wishing you were operating under different conditions? Treating each day as a gift from God means living with gratitude, intention, and awareness of His presence, recognizing that every day is an opportunity to love, grow, and glorify Him regardless of what that day looks like.

Thinking Positive Thoughts

"What about this day is a cause for celebration?" Asking yourself this question just might be the key to changing your attitude. Though our struggles and grievances tend to get more of our attention, the small joys and everyday privileges of life become cause for celebration when intentionally considered.

Remember This

Today and every day, no matter what the day looks like, try to take time to celebrate another day of life. Instead of rushing through tasks, pause and breathe. Notice the beauty in creation, the kindness in others, or any quiet nudges from the Holy Spirit. These moments remind you that God is near—today, tomorrow, and always.

Jesus intended for us to be overwhelmed by the blessings of regular days. He said it was the reason he had come: "I am come that they might have life, and that they might have it more abundantly."

GLORIA GAITHER

88

Walking with Christ

Then he said to the crowd, "If any of you wants to be my follower, you must give up your own way, take up your cross daily, and follow me."

Luke 9:23 NLT

When we turn our lives over to God's only begotten Son, we feel the sense that He is inviting us to walk with Him. To tread life's road with Jesus means living in close, daily relationship with Him—following His lead, learning from His Word, and trusting His presence amid every step of life.

Friends walk together. They share the road they're travelling, as well as their destination. The path may have its peaks and valleys, its rough patches and smooth, but walking with Jesus means never walking alone. We trust His timing, His ways, and His promises, even when the path before us is uncertain.

As we walk with Jesus, He gently transforms us. Through our conversations and shared experiences, we learn from Him, collect His wisdom, and apply it. We begin to let go of selfishness, fear, and pride and grow into the women He created us to be. And as we observe His daily example, we learn how to worship, love, and obey God and how to love and care for our neighbors.

Ultimately, if we walk alongside Jesus, we will be asked to take up our burdens and crosses—to be accompanied by the eternal blessings of following our Lord. Today let's make certain we are joining Jesus on the path He has planned for us. Could we ever ask for a better traveling companion?

Thinking Positive Thoughts

Have you ever tried traveling alone? It can be lonesome as well as difficult, especially if you're traveling long distances. But Jesus already knows the road—its high and low points, its curves, and its potholes. He is a Helper and a Guide in addition to a wonderful and trustworthy Friend. Life's journey with Him is the most faithful, joyful, and secure walk you'll ever take.

Remember This

Following Christ is a daily journey of prayer and listening. Just as walking with a friend involves conversation, walking with Jesus means talking with Him regularly, sharing your thoughts, waiting for His guidance, and inviting Him into all areas of life.

Walking with Christ is a journey, not a destination.
Keep pressing forward, even when it's hard.

Nichole Nordeman

89

Praising God Throughout the Day

In all your ways acknowledge Him,
And He shall direct your paths.

Proverbs 3:6 NKJV

How often do you find yourself thanking God for who He is and what He has done? Though we tend to think about praise as an act reserved for worship within the four walls of a church, praise can also be a soul posture that honors God in all things. Praising God throughout the day means living with a heart of gratitude, wonder, and awareness of His presence. The effort doesn't need to be formal or official; we can experience it amid our quiet rhythms and routines.

Sometimes we simply don't stop long enough to pause and thank our Creator for the countless blessings He has bestowed upon us. But when we slow down and express our gratitude to the One who made us, we enrich our own lives and the lives of those around us. Even more, we find ourselves feeling closer to God when we cultivate such patterns of praise.

To encourage a spirit of worship, endeavor to begin and end your day with a short prayer. Or consider making a list of God's blessings and adding to it whenever a new one comes to mind or reveals itself. Listen to praise music while doing everyday tasks—washing dishes, driving, paying bills—and thank God for His faithfulness as you do. Even more simply, whisper a short praise like, "You are good," or "Thank You for being with me." These small habits become sacred when you incorporate them into your day, and over time, you may feel yourself more naturally praising the name of your heavenly Father.

Thinking Positive Thoughts

Because of God's promises, we have hope in the priceless gifts of eternal love and eternal life. Despite the enormity of these blessings, praising God throughout the day doesn't require perfection or performance from us—just a willing, thankful heart that keeps turning toward Him a little at a time. As you do, praise becomes not just a task to accomplish but a way of life.

Remember This

Praise lifts your spirits, resets your perspective, and brings you closer to God. It is one of the most life-giving habits you can cultivate. It transforms how you see your circumstances, your relationships, and even yourself. It doesn't require a specific setting or a certain amount of time—only a heart that is attentive to God's presence and willing to respond with gratitude, awe, and love.

True praise comes from a heart
that is fully surrendered to God and His will.

Kari Jobe

90

Accepting God's Gift of Eternal Life

For God so loved the world that He gave His only begotten Son, that whoever believes in Him should not perish but have everlasting life.

John 3:16 NKJV

Jesus is not only the light of the world; He is also its salvation. He came to this earth, was crucified, and rose again so we might not perish but instead spend eternity with Him. What a glorious gift; what a priceless opportunity. Words cannot adequately describe what Christ's sacrifice has accomplished for humankind.

As mere humans, we can only imagine the incredible scope, and thus the value, of eternal life. Our vision of what's to come is limited, but God knows all things, sees all things, and has personally prepared a place for those who love Him and find their salvation through His Son Jesus Christ.

If you haven't already done so, this is the perfect moment to acknowledge your need for a Savior and accept the magnificent gift provided you through Christ Jesus. We all fall short of God's perfect standard (Romans 3:23), so no number of good deeds can make us right with God. But eternal life in heaven comes through faith in Jesus—believing He is the Son of God who died for your sins and rose again. His sacrifice on the cross paid the debt we couldn't pay, and His resurrection opened the door to new life.

Eternal life isn't just about going to heaven someday; it's about knowing and walking with Jesus today. Through Jesus, peace, freedom, and joy begin the moment we say yes to His salvation—the most precious gift we can enjoy each day, from now and through eternity.

Thinking Positive Thoughts

What is more encouraging than knowing your future is secure? God has already made possible life abundant and life eternal. If you have not accepted His gift, why delay? And if you have already accepted the glorious gift of His redemption, why not share that good news with someone else today?

Remember This

God has offered you life abundant and life eternal. Living abundantly and with a mind looking toward eternity means living with purpose, peace, and fullness of heart that comes from knowing you are deeply loved, fully forgiven, and eternally secure in Christ.

I can still hardly believe it. I, with shriveled, bent fingers, atrophied muscles, gnarled knees, and no feeling from the shoulders down, will one day have a new body—light, bright and clothed in righteousness—powerful and dazzling.

Joni Eareckson Tada

More from God's Word

Bible Verses Arranged by Topic

Abundance

The thief's purpose is to steal and kill and destroy. My purpose is to give them a rich and satisfying life.

John 10:10 NLT

Give, and you will receive. Your gift will return to you in full—pressed down, shaken together to make room for more, running over, and poured into your lap. The amount you give will determine the amount you get back.

Luke 6:38 NLT

And God will generously provide all you need. Then you will always have everything you need and plenty left over to share with others.

2 Corinthians 9:8 NLT

The master was full of praise. "Well done, my good and faithful servant. You have been faithful in handling this small amount, so now I will give you many more responsibilities. Let's celebrate together!"

MATTHEW 25:21 NLT

I am the Alpha and the Omega—the Beginning and the End. To all who are thirsty I will give freely from the springs of the water of life.

REVELATION 21:6 NLT

For the LORD is good. His unfailing love continues forever, and his faithfulness continues to each generation.

PSALM 100:5 NLT

No, I will not abandon you as orphans—I will come to you.

JOHN 14:18 NLT

Adversity

God blesses those who patiently endure testing and temptation. Afterward they will receive the crown of life that God has promised to those who love him.

James 1:12 NLT

Are any of you suffering hardships? You should pray..

James 5:13 NLT

They do not fear bad news; they confidently trust the Lord to care for them. They are confident and fearless and can face their foes triumphantly.

Psalm 112:7–8 NLT

The Lord *lifts up those who are weighed down.*
The Lord *loves the godly.*

Psalm 146:8 NLT

But the salvation of the righteous is from the Lord*;*
He is their strength in the time of trouble.

Psalm 37:39 NKJV

God is our refuge and strength,
always ready to help in times of trouble.
So we will not fear when earthquakes come
and the mountains crumble into the sea.

Psalm 46:1–2 NLT

The Lord *is a shelter for the oppressed,*
a refuge in times of trouble.
Those who know your name trust in you,
for you, O Lord*, do not abandon those who search for you.*

Psalm 9:9–10 NLT

Anger

Get rid of all bitterness, rage, anger, harsh words, and slander, as well as all types of evil behavior. Instead, be kind to each other, tenderhearted, forgiving one another, just as God through Christ has forgiven you.

Ephesians 4:31–32 NLT

Control your temper,
for anger labels you a fool.

Ecclesiastes 7:9 NLT

If anyone claims, "I am living in the light,"
but hates a fellow believer,
that person is still living in darkness.

1 John 2:9 NLT

People with understanding control their anger;
a hot temper shows great foolishness..
PROVERBS 14:29 NLT

Sensible people control their temper;
they earn respect by overlooking wrongs.
PROVERBS 19:11 NLT

An angry person starts fights;
a hot-tempered person commits all kinds of sin.
PROVERBS 29:22 NLT

Stop being angry! Turn from your rage!
Do not lose your temper—it only leads to harm.
PSALM 37:8 NLT

Anxiety and Worry

Worry weighs a person down.

Proverbs 12:25 NLT

So don't worry about tomorrow, for tomorrow will bring its own worries. Today's trouble is enough for today.

Matthew 6:34 NLT

The Lord is my light and my salvation—
so why should I be afraid? The Lord is my fortress,
protecting me from danger, so why should I tremble?

Psalm 27:1 NLT

Even when I walk through the darkest valley,
I will not be afraid, for you are close beside me.
Your rod and your staff protect and comfort me.

Psalm 23:4 NLT

For the Lord your God is living among you.
He is a mighty savior. He will take delight in you with great gladness. With his love, he will calm all your fears.
He will rejoice over you with joyful songs.

Zephaniah 3:17 NLT

Give your burdens to the Lord, and he will take care of you.
He will not permit the godly to slip and fall.

Psalm 55:22 NLT

When doubts filled my mind, your comfort gave me renewed hope and cheer.

Psalm 94:19 NLT

Look at the lilies and how they grow. They don't work or make their clothing, yet Solomon in all his glory was not dressed as beautifully as they are. And if God cares so wonderfully for flowers that are here today and thrown into the fire tomorrow, he will certainly care for you.

Luke 12:27–28 NLT

Celebration

Always be full of joy in the Lord.
I say it again—rejoice!
Philippians 4:4 NLT

For the happy heart,
life is a continual feast.
Proverbs 15:15 NLT

You will show me the way of life,
granting me the joy of your presence
and the pleasures of living with you forever.
Psalm 16:11 NLT

The thief's purpose is to steal and kill and destroy.
My purpose is to give them a rich and satisfying life.
JOHN 10:10 NLT

Shout with joy to the LORD, all the earth!
Worship the LORD with gladness.
Come before him, singing with joy.
PSALM 100:1–2 NLT

This is the day the LORD has made.
We will rejoice and be glad in it.
PSALM 118:24 NLT

Weeping may last through the night,
but joy comes with the morning.
PSALM 30:5 NLT

Courage

Be strong and courageous, and do the work.
Don't be afraid or discouraged,
for the Lord God, my God, is with you.
He will not fail you or forsake you.

1 Chronicles 28:20 NLT

Be on guard. Stand firm in the faith.
Be courageous. Be strong.

1 Corinthians 16:13 NLT

For God has not given us a spirit of fear and timidity,
but of power, love, and self-discipline.

2 Timothy 1:7 NLT

So we can say with confidence,
"The LORD is my helper, so I will have no fear.
What can mere people do to me?"

HEBREWS 13:6 NLT

Don't be afraid, for I am with you. Don't be discouraged,
for I am your God. I will strengthen you and help you.
I will hold you up with my victorious right hand.

ISAIAH 41:10 NLT

They do not fear bad news; they confidently trust
the LORD to care for them. They are confident
and fearless and can face their foes triumphantly.

PSALM 112:7–8 NLT

A final word: Be strong in the Lord and in his mighty power

EPHESIANS 6:10 NLT

Encouragement

Encourage each other. Live in harmony and peace. Then the God of love and peace will be with you.

2 Corinthians 13:11 NLT

You must warn each other every day, while it is still "today," so that none of you will be deceived by sin and hardened against God.

Hebrews 3:13 NLT

Kind words are like honey—sweet to the soul and healthy for the body.

Proverbs 16:24 NLT

As iron sharpens iron, so a friend sharpens a friend.

Proverbs 27:17 NLT

May God, who gives this patience and encouragement,
help you live in complete harmony with each other,
as is fitting for followers of Christ Jesus.

Romans 15:5 NLT

Timely advice is lovely,
like golden apples in a silver basket.

Proverbs 25:11 NLT

So then, let us aim for harmony
in the church and try to build each other up.

Romans 14:19 NLT

Don't fret because of evildoers;
don't envy the wicked.
PROVERBS 24:19 NLT

You must not covet your neighbor's house.
You must not covet your neighbor's wife,
male or female servant, ox or donkey,
or anything else that belongs to your neighbor.
EXODUS 20:17 NLT

Let us not become conceited, or provoke one another,
or be jealous of one another.
GALATIANS 5:26 NLT

Don't envy evil people; or desire their company.
PROVERBS 24:1 NLT

Surely resentment destroys the fool,
and jealousy kills the simple.
JOB 5:2 NLT

For this is how God loved the world: He gave his one and only Son, so that everyone who believes in him will not perish but have eternal life.

John 3:16 NLT

And this world is fading away, along with everything that people crave. But anyone who does what pleases God will live forever.

1 John 2:17 NLT

For it is my Father's will that all who see his Son and believe in him should have eternal life. I will raise them up at the last day.

John 6:40 NLT

And Christ lives within you, so even though your body will die because of sin, the Spirit gives you life because you have been made right with God.

Romans 8:10 NLT

The power of the life-giving Spirit has freed you from the power of sin that leads to death.

Romans 8:2 NLT

Faith

Look at the proud! They trust in themselves,
and their lives are crooked.
But the righteous will live by their faithfulness to God.

Habakkuk 2:4 NLT

Let us hold tightly without wavering to the hope we affirm,
for God can be trusted to keep his promise.

Hebrews 10:23 NLT

And it is impossible to please
God without faith. Anyone who wants to come
to him must believe that God exists and that
he rewards those who sincerely seek him.

Hebrews 11:6 NLT

Give your burdens to the Lord, and he will take care of you. He will not permit the godly to slip and fall.

Psalm 55:22 NLT

Jesus turned around, and when he saw her he said, "Daughter, be encouraged! Your faith has made you well." And the woman was healed at that moment.

Matthew 9:22 NLT

So faith comes from hearing, that is, hearing the Good News about Christ.

Romans 10:17 NLT

Anything is possible if a person believes.

Mark 9:23 NLT

Forgiveness

Get rid of all bitterness, rage, anger, harsh words, and slander, as well as all types of evil behavior. Instead, be kind to each other, tenderhearted, forgiving one another, just as God through Christ has forgiven you.

Ephesians 4:31–32 NLT

If anyone claims, "I am living in the light,"
but hates a fellow believer,
that person is still living in darkness.

1 John 2:9 NLT

Be kind to each other, tenderhearted, forgiving one another, just as God through Christ has forgiven you.

Ephesians 4:32 NLT

Do not judge others, and you will not be judged.
Do not condemn, or it will all come back against you.
Forgive others, you will be forgiven.

Luke 6:37 NLT

But when you are praying, first forgive anyone
you are holding a grudge against, so that your
Father in heaven will forgive your sins, too.

Mark 11:25 NLT

Then Peter came to him and asked, "Lord, how often
should I forgive someone who sins against me?
Seven times?" "No , not seven times,"
Jesus replied, "but seventy times seven!

Matthew 18:21–22 NLT

Sensible people control their temper;
they earn respect by overlooking wrongs.

Proverbs 19:11 NLT

God's Guidance

Morning by morning he wakens me and opens my understanding to his will. The Sovereign L*ORD has spoken to me, and I have listened.*

ISAIAH 50:4–5 NLT

And yet, L*ORD, you are our Father. We are the clay, and you are the potter. We are all formed by your hand.*

ISAIAH 64:8 NLT

When people do not accept divine guidance, they run wild. But whoever obeys the law is joyful.

PROVERBS 29:18 NLT

Search me, O God, and know my heart; test me and know my anxious thoughts. Point out anything in me that offends you, and lead me along the path of everlasting life.

Psalm 139:23–24 NLT

The Lord says, "I will guide you along the best pathway for your life. I will advise you and watch over you."

Psalm 32:8 NLT

Trust in the Lord with all your heart; do not depend on your own understanding. Seek his will in all you do, and he will show you which path to take.

Proverbs 3:5–6 NLT

The wise are glad to be instructed.

Proverbs 10:8 NLT

God's Plan

The Lord will work out his plans for my life—
for your faithful love, O Lord, endures forever.
Psalm 138:8 NLT

Those who listen to instruction will prosper;
those who trust the Lord will be joyful.
Proverbs 16:20 NLT

We can make our plans,
but the Lord determines our steps.
Proverbs 16:9 NLT

For God is working in you, giving you the desire and the power to do what pleases him.

Philippians 2:13 NLT

The Lord directs the steps of the godly. He delights in every detail of their lives. Though they stumble, they will never fall, for the Lord *holds them by the hand.*

Psalm 37:23–24 NLT

The Lord is good and does what is right; he shows the proper path to those who go astray.

Psalm 25:8 NLT

You will show me the way of life, granting me the joy of your presence and the pleasures of living with you forever.

Psalm 16:11 NLT

God's Protection

Be strong and courageous, and do the work.
Don't be afraid or discouraged,
for the Lord *God, my God, is with you.*
He will not fail you or forsake you.

1 Chronicles 28:20 NLT

And through your faith, God is protecting you by his power until you receive this salvation, which is ready to be revealed on the last day for all to see.

1 Peter 1:5 NLT

But the Lord is faithful; he will strengthen you and guard you from the evil one.

2 Thessalonians 3:3 NLT

Don't be afraid, for I am with you. Don't be discouraged, for I am your God. I will strengthen you and help you. I will hold you up with my victorious right hand.

Isaiah 41:10 NLT

For the Lord watches over the path of the godly, but the path of the wicked leads to destruction.

Psalm 1:6 NLT

The Lord is my rock, my fortress and my savior; my God is my rock in whom I find protection. He is my shield, the power that saves me, and my place of safety.

Psalm 18:2 NLT

For the Lord your God is living among you. He is a mighty savior. He will take delight in you with gladness. With his love, he will calm all your fears. He will rejoice over you with joyful songs."

Zephaniah 3:17 NLT

Happiness

Those who listen to instruction will prosper;
those who trust the Lord will be joyful.
PROVERBS 16:20 NLT

A cheerful heart is good medicine,
but a broken spirit saps a person's strength.
PROVERBS 17:22 NLT

Joyful is the person who finds wisdom
the one gains understanding.
PROVERBS 3:13 NLT

How joyful are those who fear the LORD *and delight in obeying his commands..*
PSALM 112:1 NLT

What joy for those who can live in your house, always singing your praises. What joy for those whose strength comes from the Lord.

Psalm 84:4–5 NLT

I will praise you, Lord, with all my heart; I will tell of all the marvelous things you have done.
I will be filled with joy because of you.
I will sing praises to your name, O Most High.

Psalm 9:1–2 NLT

Happy are those who hear the joyful call to worship, for they will walk in the light of your presence, Lord.

Psalm 89:15 NLT

This is the day the Lord has made.
We will rejoice and be glad in it.

Psalm 118:24 NLT

*Let us hold tightly without wavering
to the hope we affirm, for God
can be trusted to keep his promise.*

HEBREWS 10:23 NLT

*I say to myself, "The LORD is my inheritance;
therefore, I will hope in him!"*

LAMENTATIONS 3:24 NLT

*But joyful are those . . . whose hope
is in the LORD their God.*

PSALM 146:5 NLT

*So each generation should set its hope anew
on God, not forgetting his glorious miracles
and obeying his commands.*

PSALM 78:7 NLT

*The fears of the wicked will be fulfilled;
the hopes of the godly will be granted.*

PROVERBS 10:24 NLT

Love

Dear friends, since God loved us that much, we surely ought to love each other.

1 John 4:11 NLT

Love each other deeply with all your heart.

1 Peter 1:22 NLT

Live a life filled with love, following the example of Christ. He loved us and offered himself as a sacrifice for us, a pleasing aroma to God..

Ephesians 5:2 NLT

Love is patient and kind. Love is not jealous or boastful or proud.

1 Corinthians 13:4 NLT

Above all, clothe yourselves with love, which binds us all together in perfect harmony.

Colossians 3:14 NLT

Obedience

And this world is fading away, along with everything that people crave. But anyone who does what pleases God will live forever..

1 John 2:17 NLT

But Samuel replied, "What is more pleasing to the Lord: your burnt offerings and sacrifices or your obedience to his voice? Listen! Obedience is better than sacrifice, and submission is better than offering the fat of rams.

1 Samuel 15:22 NLT

But if you look carefully into the perfect law that sets you free, and if you do what it says and don't forget what you heard, then God will bless you for doing it.

James 1:25 NLT

Jesus replied, "Who is my mother? Who are my brothers?" Then he looked at those around him and said, "Look, these are my mother and brothers. Anyone who does God's will is my brother and sister and mother."

Mark 3:33–35 NLT

No, O people, the Lord has told you what is good, and this is what he requires of you: to do what is right, to love mercy, and to walk humbly with your God.

Micah 6:8 NLT

Anyone who listens to my teaching and follows it is wise, like a person who builds a house on solid rock.

Matthew 7:24 NLT

For God is working in you, giving you the desire and the power to do what pleases him.

Philippians 2:13 NLT

Patience

And knowledge with self-control,
and self-control with patient endurance,
and patient endurance with godliness.
2 Peter 1:6 NLT

Finishing is better than starting.
Patience is better than pride.
Ecclesiastes 7:8 NLT

Patient endurance is what you need now,
so that you will continue to do God's will.
Then you will receive all that he has promised.
Hebrews 10:36 NLT

Better to be patient than powerful; better to have self-control than to conquer a city.

Proverbs 16:32 NLT

Wait patiently for the Lord. Be brave and courageous. Yes, wait patiently for the Lord.

Psalm 27:14 NLT

Put your hope in the Lord.
Travel steadily along his path. He will honor you.

Psalm 37:34 NLT

The Lord is good to those who depend on him, to those who search for him. So it is good to wait quietly for salvation from the Lord.

Lamentations 3:25–26 NLT

Praise

Enter his gates with thanksgiving; go into his courts with praise. Give thanks to him and praise his name. For the L*ORD* *is good. His unfailing love continues forever, and his faithfulness continues to each generation.*

PSALM 100:4–5 NLT

The Lord is my strength and my song; he has given me victory. This is my God, and I will praise him.

EXODUS 15:2 NLT

I will praise the LORD *at all times.*
I will constantly speak his praises.

PSALM 34:1 NLT

I will praise you, Lord, with all my heart;
I will tell of all the marvelous things you have done.
I will be filled with joy because of you.
I will sing praises to your name, O Most High.

Psalm 9:1–2 NLT

Praise the Lord, all you nations. Praise him, all you people of the earth. For his unfailing love for us is powerful; the Lord's faithfulness endures forever. Praise the Lord!

Psalm 117 NLT

Great is the Lord! He is most worthy of praise!
No one can measure his greatness.

Psalm 145:3 NLT

Everywhere—from east to west—
praise the name of the Lord.

Psalm 113:3 NLT

Prayer

The earnest prayer of a righteous person has great power and produces wonderful results.

James 5:16 NLT

But when you are praying, first forgive anyone you are holding a grudge against, so that your Father in heaven will forgive your sins, too.

Mark 11:25 NLT

One day Jesus told his disciples a story to show that they should always pray and never give up.

Luke 18:1 NLT

Your Father knows exactly what you need even before you ask him!

Matthew 6:8 NLT

Then if my people who are called by my name will humble themselves and pray and seek my face and turn from their wicked ways, I will hear from heaven and will forgive their sins and restore their land.

2 Chronicles 7:14 NLT

Are any of you suffering hardships?
You should pray.

James 5:13 NLT

May the words of my mouth and the meditation of my heart be pleasing to you,
O Lord, my rock and my redeemer.

Psalm 19:14 NLT

Spiritual Growth

When I was a child, I spoke and thought
and reasoned as a child.
But when I grew up, I put away childish things.

1 Corinthians 13:11 NLT

Grow in the grace and knowledge of
our Lord and Savior Jesus Christ.
All glory to him, both now and forever! Amen.

2 Peter 3:18 NLT

So let us stop going over the basic teachings
about Christ again and again. Let us go on
instead and become mature in our understanding.

Hebrews 6:1 NLT

I remind you to fan into flames
the spiritual gift God gave you.

2 Timothy 1:6 NLT

Leave your simple ways behind,
and begin to live; learn to use good judgment.

Proverbs 9:6 NLT

For God is working in you, giving you the desire
and the power to do what pleases him.

Philippians 2:13 NLT

Don't copy the behavior and customs of this world,
but let God transform you into a new person
by changing the way you think. Then you will learn
to know God's will for you, which is
good and pleasing and perfect.

Romans 12:2 NLT

Strength

Be strong and courageous, and do the work.
Don't be afraid or discouraged,
for the LORD God, my God, is with you.
He will not fail you or forsake you.

1 CHRONICLES 28:20 NLT

The Lord is my strength and my song; he has become
given me victory. This is my God, and I will praise him.

EXODUS 15:2 NLT

For the Kingdom of God is not just a lot of talk;
it is living by God's power.

1 CORINTHIANS 4:20 NLT

Do not be afraid or discouraged.
For the LORD your God is with you wherever you go.

JOSHUA 1:9 NLT

Don't be afraid, for I am with you. Don't be discouraged, for I am your God. I will strengthen you and help you. I will hold you up with my victorious right hand.

Isaiah 41:10 NLT

Be on guard. Stand firm in the faith. Be courageous. Be strong.

1 Corinthians 16:13 NLT

But those who trust in the Lord will find new strength. They will soar high on wings like eagles. They will run and not grow weary. They will walk and not faint.

Isaiah 40:31 NLT

A final word: Be strong in the Lord and in his mighty power.

Ephesians 6:10 NLT

Trusting God

Those who trust in the Lord are as secure as Mount Zion; they will not be defeated but will endure forever.

Psalm 125:1 NLT

Those who listen to instruction will prosper; those who trust the Lord will be joyful.

Proverbs 16:20 NLT

O Lord, I give my life to you. I trust in you, my God!

Psalm 25:1–2 NLT

Many sorrows come to the wicked, but unfailing love surrounds those who trust the LORD.

PSALM 32:10 NLT

Commit everything you do to the LORD.
Trust him, and he will help you.

PSALM 37:5 NLT

The LORD is my rock, my fortress, and my savior; my God is my rock, in whom I find protection. He is my shield, the power that saves me, and my place of safety.

PSALM 18:2 NLT

Trust in the LORD with all your heart; do not depend on your own understanding. Seek his will in all you do, and he will show you which path to take.

PROVERBS 3:5–6 NLT

1. Air1 Afternoons**,** "Lauren & Tasha Layton Talk About the Power of Prayer," YouTube video, 0:10:56, accessed July 14, 2025, https://www.youtube.com/watch?v=uo3JSgXS3bU&t=656s.

2. Sarah H. Bradford and J. Mitchell, MA, *Tubman's Underground Rail: Her Paths to Freedom. Guided by Harriet Tubman also known as the Moses of Her People. With Scenes from Her Life. An Original Compilation* (Lulu.com, November 30, 2017).

3. Reader's Digest Editors, "Real Miracles That Make Life Worth Living," Reader's Digest, updated September 1, 2023, https://www.rd.com/list/real-miracles/

4. That Sounds Fun, "CeCe Winans on the Holy Spirit, Perseverance, and Building Legacy | That Sounds Fun Podcast #465," YouTube video, 0:38:24, May 1, 2023, accessed July 14, 2025, https://www.

5. Jesus Calling Podcast, "Our Dreams, God's Calling: Jaci Velasquez and Andy Harrison," YouTube video, 0:28:31, July 16, 2020, accessed July 14, 2025, https://www.youtube.com/

6. Jill Gleeson, "The 25 Best Rosa Parks Quotes About Social Justice and Equality," *Country Living*, January 18, 2024, https://www.countryliving.com/life/a46353973/rosa-parks-quotes/.

7. Praise on TBN, "Priscilla Shirer: You're Right Where You Need to Be | FULL SERMON | TBN," YouTube video, 0:37:36, April 22, 2024, accessed July 14, 2025, https://www.youtube.com/

8. Women of Faith on TBN, "Mandisa: Prayer Saved My Life | Women of Faith on TBN," YouTube video, January 11, 2023, accessed July 14, 2025,

9. Hope On Demand, "Following God Even When You're Unsure – Madison Cain Johnson," YouTube video, accessed July 14, 2025, https://www.youtube.

10. Rebecca St. James, foreword to *Loved: Stories of Forgiveness*, by Rebecca St. James (FaithWords, 2009).

11. *The ClingLife Show with Kim Cash Tate, "Wait for the Lord. It's Not Too Late," YouTube video, accessed July 14, 2025,* https://www.youtube.com/

12. YouVersion, "Christine Caine | James 1:5," Facebook video, n.d., accessed July 14, 2025, https://www.facebook.com/YouVersion/videos/

13. Anne Wilson, *My Jesus: From Heartache to Hope* (Thomas Nelson, 2022), 121.

14. Ruth Chou Simons, *Now and Not Yet: Pressing in When You're Waiting, Wanting, and Restless for More* (Thomas Nelson, April 9, 2024), 119.

15. *Lisa Sharon Harper, The Very Good Gospel: How Everything Wrong Can Be Made Right* (Crown Publishing Group, 2016), 72.

16. Ellie Holcomb, *Fighting Words Journaling Devotional: 100 Days of Speaking Truth into the Darkness* (B&H Books, 2021), 12.

17. Ann Voskamp, *One Thousand Gifts: A Dare to Live Fully Right Where You Are* (Zondervan, 2010), 48.